THE MINISTRY OF THE WORD

The Ministry of the Word

R. E. C. BROWNE

SCM PRESS LTD

334 01009 8
First published 1958
by SCM Press Ltd
26–30 Tottenham Road, London N1 4BZ
Reissued 1976
Second impression 1984
Printed in Great Britain by
Richard Clay (The Chaucer Press) Ltd
Bungay, Suffolk

CONTENTS

Acknowledgments   7

Foreword by Ronald Preston   9

1   The Vocation of a Minister of the Word   15

2   Preacher and Poet – an Analogy   23

3   Authority   32

4   The Exposition of Doctrine   41

5   A Note on Theological 'Schizophrenia'   51

6   The Essential Untidiness   58

7   What is Communicated?   72

8   The Use of Images   82

9   A Personal Form   91

10 Some Observations on the Modern Situation   101

11 Modern Apologetics   114

12 Word and Sacrament   124

Index   128

ACKNOWLEDGMENTS

We gratefully acknowledge permission of the following to quote from copyright material:

Faber & Faber Ltd and Harcourt Brace Jovanovich Inc. for permission to quote extracts from 'Four Quartets' and 'Chorus from "The Rock"' from *Collected Poems 1909–1962*, and from *The Cocktail Party*, by T. S. Eliot.

Faber & Faber Ltd and Random House Inc. for permission to quote from the two poems by W. H. Auden from his *Collected Longer Poems*.

Mr Robert Graves for permission to quote his poem 'In Broken Images', taken from his *Collected Poems*, Cassell and Doubleday & Co. Inc. 1975.

Macmillan & Co. and David Higham Associates Ltd for permission to quote from 'In the Night' from *Collected Poems 1967* by Elizabeth Jennings.

The Society of Authors as the literary representative of the Estate of A. E. Housman and Jonathan Cape Ltd and Holt, Rinehart & Winston Inc., publishers of A. E. Housman's *Collected Poems*, for permission to quote from 'They say my verse is sad: no wonder'.

Curtis Brown Ltd, on behalf of Mr John Wain, for permission to quote from 'Who Speaks My Language' from *New Lines, An Anthology* ed. Robert Conquest, published by Macmillan & Co.

FOREWORD

THIS short book is a little masterpiece both in depth of thought and quality of expression. I thought so when it was first published in 1958. I read it three or four times within six months of its publication, something I had never done with any other book and have never done since. The passage of time has confirmed my immediate reaction, not least because many others whose judgments I respect have shared my appreciation of it. It has been out of print for some years. I have never seen a second-hand copy for sale, and I know several people who have been trying for a long time to obtain one for themselves and have not succeeded. Others would have liked to recommend it to students but have not felt able to do so because of the difficulty of securing copies. I am therefore very pleased that the SCM Press has decided to re-issue *The Ministry of the Word*; and as one of those who was fortunate enough to be a friend of Charlie Browne for nearly thirty years, I am grateful for the opportunity to write an introductory note about him and this book.

The outward facts of the life of Robert Eric Charles Browne are soon told. He graduated from Trinity College, Dublin, in 1928 (where he was a contemporary of another master of words, Samuel Beckett), and was ordained in the Church of Ireland, serving successively in the parishes of St Luke and St Thomas, Belfast, for a total of thirteen years before becoming Chaplain to St Columba's College, near Dublin, the well-known boarding school for boys. From there he came to England just after the war as Secretary to the Theological Colleges Department of the Student Christian Movement. Based upon London, this job involved much travelling over the whole of the British Isles. He was more senior than most members of SCM staff, and his unusual range of experience and depths of pastoral insight were of great value not only to his colleagues but to the students and members of staff, and not least the Principals, of the Theological Colleges he visited. In 1949 he came to Manchester as Rector of All Saints, West Gorton, an industrial parish near the famous Manchester popular entertainment centre Belle Vue. (It has now been amalgamated with another parish, and in the reorganization the previous churches have been demolished and a new one built with a new dedication.) From there he became Rector of St Chrysostom,

Victoria Park, Manchester, from which ill-health compelled him to retire in 1959. Victoria Park is an area of great social interest in Manchester, which has moved rapidly since the 1920s from the remains of enclosed and privileged nineteenth-century affluence to near disintegration. An excellent impression of it as it was can be found in the first few pages of Neville Cardus' autobiography; and it is the subject of a detailed study shortly to be issued by the Chetham Society and Manchester University Press.[1] St Chrysostom's is a difficult parish from which to secure a regular and stable congregation, but it is conveniently near the university and its main teaching hospital, and from this base the influence of Charlie Browne began to spread unobtrusively but widely. The local branch of the William Temple Association (made up of young Christian university graduates working in Manchester) drew most of its inspiration from him; and when in the end it was decided to hold a Wake to mark the demise of the branch because Charlie Browne thought its members needed a less structured activity, the Wake was such a success that one was held every month for several years!

The illness which brought about his early retirement was Parkinson's disease. At first his ministry was even more fruitful on retirement than in a parish. Freed from tasks which were becoming physically harder to accomplish, he could concentrate on what he could still do comparatively unhindered as confessor and as pastoral counsellor in the widest sense and with very varied types of people in age, sex, and occupation. I mention those aspects which I knew best. Bishops of different dioceses sent clergy in difficulties to him for pastoral care. In the Manchester diocese he continued to be a tower of strength in post-ordination work with junior clergy, partly by his fertility of mind and wise advice, partly as tutor to those who wished to be guided in 'clinical theology' (a term then coming into vogue), and who came to him singly and in small groups.

The disease slowly grew worse. When he was made an Honorary Canon of Manchester Cathedral in 1964 movement was so difficult for him that he had to be installed quietly one weekday morning, and I don't think he ever entered the Cathedral again. His speech became affected and that, coupled with his soft southern Irish tone of voice, made it increasingly difficult to hear what he said. Moreover, although his mind remained as active as ever, he could not co-ordinate his thoughts with physical movement either to dictate them or to write them down himself.

[1] Maurice Spiers, *Victoria Park, Manchester – A Nineteenth Century Suburb*.

As this book makes clear, language was a pre-occupation and a delight to him. He savoured poetry and drama and tried his hand at both. A play of his was produced by Pamela Keily in Manchester Diocese, and one of his poems was read at his funeral. He also painted. He was one of the best read people I have known. It is impossible not to regret the books he had it in him to write but which the cruel disease prevented him writing. Towards the end he lost the power of speech and almost the power of movement. He was a big man in stature and had been a considerable athlete in his youth, but he became a silent shrunken figure in a prison.

His friends rejoiced when he married in 1948, and he and Mary Browne forged a deeply happy marriage in the course of which he became almost totally dependent on her. Her care for every detail enabled his ministry to continue much longer than would otherwise have been possible. When it became no longer possible to move him single-handed he was received into St Ann's Hospice, a terminal hospital just south of Manchester, whose establishment was the last of Bishop Greer's initiatives before his retirement as Bishop of Manchester. (It was Bishop Greer who had brought Charlie Brown to the Diocese.) He spent the last six months of his life excellently nursed in St Ann's Hospice, and even then, although speechless and almost helpless, in an extraordinary way he was a means of blessing to many of the patients and nursing staff. But no one could have wished him to linger, and it was a matter of rejoicing that he died quietly on the evening of Ascension Day 1975, and that Mary Browne was there. His funeral was the most joyous I have known. He himself had a deep sense of joy and also of fun. Humorous Irish stories poured from him, and a wealth of shrewd comments upon men and events which comprehended the darkest sides of life within a charity rooted in a sense of the creative and sustaining charity of God. At his funeral Bishop Richard Hanson, another friend of long standing and, like him, a product of Anglo-Irish culture, pointed out that the cross-fertilization in this inheritance had produced qualities of mind and penetration in the use of words which are exemplified in a long tradition including Berkeley, Swift, Sheridan, Wilde, Shaw and Yeats, and it is in this tradition that we must put the intellectual contribution of Charlie Browne.

His published work is found in four brief sources. The first, *Meditations on the Temptations and Passion of our Lord*, a forty-four page booklet, was published by SCM Press in 1955, ran into a second edition in 1957, and has long been unobtainable. Charlie Browne was accustomed to write and re-write with great care (he said that sloth in a theologian is an unwillingness to write and re-write). He sent this text to the then Editor of SCM Press, Ronald Gregor Smith, in a tentative way for advice as to whether the meditations were worth further work, and was surprised to find them accepted at once and as they were for publication. They contain many good things but do not prepare us for what was to come in this present book. But before saying more about it I want to refer to his other published writings. In the years 1961–3 Dr Alec Vidler, as Editor of *Theology*, commissioned a series of eleven articles on traditional virtues, which were re-published by SPCK in 1964 under the title *Traditional Virtues Reassessed*; the sixth, on Piety, was a characteristic piece by Charlie Browne carrying echoes of Thomas Traherne. More extensive are thirty-nine articles for *A Dictionary of Christian Ethics*, published by the SCM Press in 1967. I had a certain amount to do with the preparation of this Dictionary and the best thing I did was to suggest that Charlie Browne be asked to write on various virtues and vices. He produced little gems. All told they came to about 14,000 words. The shortest, like Accidie or Remorse, total about 100 words or less; the longest, like Righteousness or Wisdom are about 700; the majority are in the 300–400 word range. He covers eighteen virtues, seventeen vices and four general topics, for example Cardinal Virtues and Saintliness.[1]

It was doubtless the exigencies of balancing contributors from different traditions and both sides of the Atlantic which accounts for the fact that Charlie Browne writes on three of the four cardinal virtues but not Justice; on one of the theological virtues (Hope) but not Faith or Love; and the collective one on Vice but not the one on Virtue. Writing *readable* articles of these lengths for a dictionary is exceedingly difficult. Every word must tell and not one be wasted. Charlie Browne's style was ideally suited to the task; concise, clear, polished, epigrammatic but not

---

[1] Since there is no list in the Dictionary of the contributions of each contributor, I add one of those by Charlie Browne: Accidie, Anger, Avarice, Blessedness, Cardinal Virtues, Childlikeness, Concupiscence, Courage, Courtesy, Covetousness, Cruelty, Envy, Gluttony, Hatred, Honesty, Honour, Hope, Hospitality, Humility, Hybris, Hypocrisy, Jealousy, Lust, Magnanimity, Malice, Meekness, Mercy, Prudence, Remorse, Repentance, Righteousness, Saintliness, Slander, Sloth, Temperance, Tolerance, Vice, Wisdom, Zeal.

smart, 'gnomic' in fact. However, it is not only a matter of style, the thought is creative. These are old themes but they have been re-thought in today's context in a manner which is truly original. In a sense they are magisterial; only one, Righteousness, refers to any other books. Moreover, even in this short compass they frequently embody quite specific illustrations (e.g. Honesty, Jealousy), and they often include not merely a personal exposition but pointed applications to the life of the church and to social groups. I can think of few more suitable sources for Lenten meditation than these articles. They are full of pithy sentences which one wants to write down and go back to again and again, and underlying them is a profound belief in the ceaseless divine creativity into which we are called and incorporated: 'Meekness is a quality of living characteristic of a man who knows he is participating in the creative activity of God, not as a pauper but as a son.'

The qualities shown in these vignettes in *A Dictionary of Christian Ethics* had been shown in *The Ministry of the Word* nine years previously on a larger but still comparatively small scale. I am not sure I have ever found so much deep thought expressed so concisely (except in St Anselm!). The title is innocuous and somewhat misleading. It is not just one more little book on sermons and preaching of the type found on second-hand book stalls. It is about the possibility of revelation itself, its authority, its appropriation and its communication, particularly by words. It involves the entire stance by which the Christian faith is apprehended, and its implications for preaching and, equally important, for listening to preaching. When it first appeared it seemed more difficult to read than it does now. This was not due to obscurity in the writing but to the new thoughts we were being asked to think, or perhaps the challenge to pursue the far reaching implications of an approach to the Christian faith which we had accepted but had not followed through, so that our practice was inconsistent with our avowed pre-suppositions (see chapter 5). Today the themes taken up by Charlie Browne have become much more in the centre of serious theological reflection. He was ahead of most of us as poets often are. And this is not surprising because he was a poet himself. His sermons were prose poems. He continually comes back in this book to the poets and frequently quotes from them; the visual arts are also constantly brought in.

There is hardly a word out of place in the whole book. It is tightly integrated. The thought again and again comes back to the same

13

themes, like that of the author of I John, ever more deeply expounded. An example is the quotation from de Burgh on p. 30 which is repeated and extended on p. 78. Yet there is space for quite detailed advice to be given at times.

The advice is not easy to practice. In some ways chapter 8, *The Use of Images*, focuses most clearly the implications of the book for the activity of preaching. Here we are told that to use images to attract attention and then plain prose to illuminate is a false policy; rather the preacher should use words to evoke images which move the mind, as the poet does. In particular sermons should not be weighed down with instruction and exhortation. The preacher should remember the words of the psalmist, often quoted by Charlie Browne: 'he telleth his dark speech upon the harp' (Ps. 49.4). I confess I have by no means come to terms with this myself as yet. Certainly Charlie Browne did not expect everyone to preach like himself. Indeed they could not, for his sermons were peculiarly characteristic of the man, as he tells us sermons should be (chapter 1). It was not easy to get 'on the wavelength' until you knew him. Things were not made easier by the soft Irish brogue and the throwaway manner in which they were delivered, lacking any artifice, which made them hard to hear. But soon you knew that it was worth using all the alertness and powers of concentration you possessed to catch what was being said.

As to preaching, Charlie Browne leaves us with the far-reaching thought that the preacher, like the biblical writers themselves, is a free agent using his imagination and intelligence in obedience to divine promptings. Further, as I have said, he draws out for us the whole cast of mind and imagination by which Christian faith can be apprehended, expressed and lived in and through a church which is open, self-critical and reflecting deeply on the faith she has received from the past in the context of our situation today. The dangers, temptations and errors to which he points are all subordinate to his positive theme. He has left us a legacy in this book which will be fruitful for several decades, and which may well survive as a classic of British twentieth-century divinity.

Faculty of Theology,   RONALD PRESTON
The University of Manchester
St Matthew's Day, 1975

14

CHAPTER ONE

THE VOCATION OF A MINISTER OF THE WORD

A MINISTER of the Word who writes about preaching writes as a learner to other learners and like them he is haunted by the sermon that no one is great enough to preach.

This book is concerned with the fact that what a preacher believes about the mode of divine revelation determines the mode of his preaching. Those who believe in the literal inspiration of the Scriptures do so by doctrines which must also govern their work as preachers. That is, those who hold that divine revelation is given in propositional form will regard preaching as the statement of doctrine in a series of propositions expressed in definable terms. In that case the inspiration of the preacher would consist in his being given the right propositions for his use according to the needs of his generation. His task would then be thought of as giving a simple message couched in unequivocal terms, making the meaning of his message clear and being ready to answer those who affirm that what he says is meaningless. What is believed about inspiration and revelation makes a particular form of sermon inevitable. Many who deny the literal inspiration of the Scriptures govern their work as preachers by doctrinal principles which assume that divine revelation is given in propositions. The form of their sermons denies implicitly what they state explicitly about the mode of revelation. The commonly used phrase 'He gets it across' and many discussions about the problem of communication show a confusion about beliefs and techniques and an unawareness of their connexion. There can be no great preaching whenever the question 'Is there a knowledge of reality which can neither be perceived nor expressed in propositional form?' is unasked or left unanswered.

Ministers of the Word who deny the literal inspiration of the Scriptures are incoherent unless they make clear to themselves the doctrinal position to which such a denial commits them. It is not enough to postulate that to preach the living Lord of life and death requires something other than the use of formulae. To postulate this provokes questions which must be considered—christological questions and questions which concern beliefs about the nature of the ceaseless activity of God without which there could be no thought or speech. Such questions must be answered according to the doctrinal principles which are taken as axiomatic when pronouncements are made about the inspiration of the Scriptures. If the biblical writers were automatic writers who transcribed at the divine dictation, then the preacher must look on his work in the same light. If the biblical writers are held to be free agents who used their imagination and intelligence in obedience to the divine promptings to say the greatest things about God and man, then the preacher must look on his work accordingly. Only thus may the preacher discover more clearly the nature of the creative effort he is to make in his work with words.

The minister of the Word is to be as diligent in the study of words as the poet and as skilful in their use. Marianne Moore[1] would probably apply to preacher as well as to poet all that she says about the need for humility, concentration and gusto in the use of words. Humility she describes as the necessary armour. By concentration she means the intensity that makes for clear language; for her, gusto is the spontaneity which humility and skill make possible. Preaching is an art; great art hides the technical ability of the artist and draws no attention to his cleverness. Great art always seems inevitable—the thing could have been said in no other way; it is exuberant and yet controlled by a strength that maintains order without force; it expresses enough to be meaningful and never more than enough. Effective ministers of the Word are not verbose, obscure or obscurantist; they do not abuse, they do not patronize and they never embarrass; they do

[1] See Marianne Moore, *Predilections*, Faber & Faber, 1956, p. 12.

not make false simplifications in the interests of being understood; they speak as plainly as their subject matter allows and as their development permits. They have sufficient mastery of their subject and of themselves to be the servants of all who will pay attention to them.

'My son, if thou wouldest come to serve the Lord, prepare thy soul to meet temptation.' The life of a minister of the Word can only be lived in the face of temptation, but the Apostle would remind him 'There hath no temptation taken you, but such as is common to man: but God is faithful who will not suffer you to be tempted above that ye are able; but will with the temptation also make a way of escape, that ye may be able to bear it.' To follow the way of escape is part of the process described by our Lord as 'losing life', which is the frightening experience of continually putting aside all that gives ease, security and importance in the world of time and space so as to walk empty-handed into the dark where movement is not without struggle, struggle intensified by streams of images and the teeming multiplicity of thoughts that populate the mind. Creative work always brings creative workers to the edge of an abyss. It is there that the most creative work is done and it is there that conditions exist which may be the undoing of the worker: passionate faith gives rise to profound doubt; love of truth dreads error, bringing one to the verge of falsehood; depth of love increases ability to hate in the name of love; zeal drives the zealous towards fanaticism; desire to influence others brings one into the danger of being enslaved by those whom he would free. Great preaching, like great art, cannot be the work of those who know no chaos within them and it cannot be the work of those who are unable to master the chaos within them.

There is need for preachers to steady one another to deal with their present common temptations. These may be indicated by noting two prevailing tendencies: first, the tendency to regard administration and other outward activity as the only genuine human work and to disregard the value of all interior activity which has no obvious connexion with overt action; secondly, the tendency to deny the value of all visible activity after either examining the agent's motives or the probable consequences of his actions. This second tendency springs from a belief in the value of interior activity for its own sake, which means that it need not, and in fact cannot, be expressed in appropriate exterior behaviour. These attitudes about interior and exterior deeds provide the occasion when a preacher is tempted to give up the hidden work of thought, study and prayer that he may give all his time and energy to visiting, arranging, planning, helping; or else he is tempted to withdraw within himself, giving up belief in the meaningfulness of overt acts because no one seems to understand what is said or done. The preacher's sermons are a most important part of his behaviour and are made as the result of an incalculable amount of hidden work. This hidden work is largely all that he does to maintain the mood in which prayer and sermon-making are possible. In the course of this kind of living, the minister of the Word knows the fruits of achievement and the desolation and agony known to all creative workers. He knows the paralysed mind when his thoughts are caught in tangles of words; he knows the urge to give up all attempt at significant speech in favour of talking trivialities or remaining silent. These states may be due to prayer-lessness or to the exhaustion of one who has not yet achieved sufficient mastery over himself in the times when he is not deliber-ately applying himself to prayer or sermon-making. Of course he does not make his mastery of himself; it is given him by God, but to receive it is real work.

Creative workers such as preachers, musicians, poets, painters are tempted in different ways at different times to retire from the struggle for coherent expression or to deny the value of what they do when they are not actively engaged in the use of their medium. Painting is not merely what a painter does when he is at the canvas with a brush in his hand; the painting arises largely through what he does when he is not painting or thinking about painting. He will think a great deal about the technique of painting and he will talk about the philosophy of painting to clarify his mind, but when he is at the canvas he will not be consciously considering questions of technique or the philosophy of art. A man cannot think and paint at the same time and do both well; at the canvas his mind is most often empty and apparently purposeless. There is a moment in all creative activity when the work becomes automatic, because the worker is possessed by a power which does not seem to be of his own making and yet could not be without his sustained effort. After the automatic moment comes the need for conscious labour, skilled, imaginative, intelligent labour. The automatic moment cannot be willed; it can be recognized and used. It comes in the course of living the style of life which differentiates creative men and women from those who are content to go on repeating what others are saying. The landscape that is a cliché, the painter saying in paint what many other painters have said, may be competently painted but the form of truth in landscape painting is other than an efficient representation of the popular idea of what a landscape ought to look like. 'Matthew Arnold condemned poetry which is no more than "a shower of isolated thoughts and images".'[1] He would also have condemned a poem that was no more than the competent repetition of a worn platitude. The significance of a painting or a poem depends on far more than technical ability, but the artist with insufficient technical ability is soon forced to repeat himself or give up. Like all artists the preacher is called to study the techniques he requires for the practice of his art. He cannot do this apart from consideration of the doctrines he is to express through his techniques—technique must be adapted to doctrine, never doctrine to technique. The preacher's task is to know doctrine in such a way that he knows life in terms of doctrine and doctrine in terms of life. T. S. Eliot says that a good poet is conscious where he should be conscious and unconscious where he should be unconscious; this is also true of the preacher and he achieves it by living a style of life which enables him to preach in such a way that his listeners are aware of his subject rather than the form of his utterance. St Augustine said 'Love God and do

[1] C. Day Lewis, *The Poetic Image*, Jonathan Cape, 1947, p. 54.

what you like.' The corollary of this for the minister of the Word is 'Be careful of all that you think and do out of the pulpit, and preach your sermons freely'.

The preacher is called to a type of life in which there is a balance between solitude and society. His solitude will be occupied with prayer, study and continual work on the meaning of words and the making of sentences. At all times he will remember that he has a professional concern for words and that his sincerity will not be maintained without regard for his exercise of this concern. No full human life can be lived in isolation and therefore the minister of the Word takes his place in society. He is a man apart but he is not to be aloof, for his ministry is his expression of love for God and for men and his best speech arises out of this love, illuminating and being illuminated by it. R. G. Collingwood's description of the vocation of an artist might well be used for reflection on the vocation of a minister of the Word. He says: "The artist must prophesy not in the sense that he foretells things to come, but in the sense that he tells his audience, at the risk of their displeasure, the secrets of their own hearts. His business as an artist is to speak out, to make a clean breast. But what he has to utter is not, as the individualist theory of art would have us think, his own secrets. As spokesman of his community, the secrets he must utter are theirs. The reason why they need him is that no community altogether knows its own heart; and by failing in this knowledge a community deceives itself on the one subject concerning which ignorance means death. For the evils which come from that ignorance the poet as prophet suggests no remedy, because he has already given one. The remedy is the poem itself. Art is the community's medicine for the worst disease of the mind, the corruption of consciousness.'[1] Collingwood explains what he means by the corruption of consciousness in this way: 'First, we direct our attention towards a certain feeling, or become conscious of it. Then we take fright at what we have recognized: not because

[1] R. G. Collingwood, *The Principles of Art*, Oxford University Press, 1938, p. 336.

the feeling, as an impression, is an alarming impression, but because the idea into which we are converting it proves an alarming idea. We cannot see our way to dominate it, and shrink from persevering in the attempt. We therefore give it up, and turn our attention to something less intimidating.'[1] Collingwood's description is not used to suggest that the minister of the Word is called to accuse and abuse. The truths of the Gospel are 'the medicine for the worst disease of the mind, the corruption of consciousness'. But although their first effect may be to make the condition worse, their final effect is other, because the Gospel has power both to enlighten and to burn. In other words, enlightenment is not without pain, and the preacher must have sufficient love to give pain and to endure pain. In the name of his master he must often use the sword and offer the sword to others. The Gospel makes men free, but often slavery seems more reasonable and more happy in its limited way.

'He that is faithful in little is faithful in much.' Preachers are not to be overconcerned with the results of their sermons; they are to give careful attention to all that makes the construction of sermons possible. Sometimes preachers show disdain for the form in which truth can be uttered, as if truth were a thing you took in the hands of your mind and mixed with other ingredients to make a sermon, not having to care what the other ingredients were or what the final mixing was like as long as truth was included. We are to labour to find the best form of words to express what should be expressed in the combination of awe and freedom which is the way that men should speak of God. It would be easy to talk smoothly of God if he were not both immanent and transcendent, omnipotent and merciful, infinitely strong and infinitely compassionate, omnipresent yet caring for each person in each place with unfailing wisdom, patience and love. It would be easy to talk smoothly and competently if it could be stated exactly what the Incarnation and the Atonement mean. A preacher could more

[1] R. G. Collingwood, *The Principles of Art*, Oxford University Press, 1938, p. 217.

easily be fluent if he had not to keep in mind the threefold nature of man: that man is a creature, finite, limited in knowledge and power; that he is made in the image of God and so capable of relationship with God; that he is a sinner and so capable of the most hideous stupidity and cruelty when he sets out to be all-powerful or sinks down to being sub-human. Not only have preachers to move men to repent; they have to do their part in making an atmosphere in which men and women may be aware of the manifold calls of God to creative activity. They have to steady men and women to receive the call of God and to believe in it when it stirs them to ignore the duties of home, friends, neighbours for an adventure that seems absurd to the secular, heartless to the sentimental, but the only thing possible to imagination and intelligence illuminated by faith. A minister of the Word is not only an agent in assuring people of the certainty of faith, he is also an agent to lead them out into the desert where no water is, where no birds sing, where wild beasts prowl. For some this leading is a call to a life of solitude; for all it means going beyond the safe outposts guarded by reason and far beyond the territory protected by earthly prudence. Here it is easy to be wrong and to lead wrongly, nevertheless the minister must run the risks that love of God and men entails—such is his calling.

There can be no conclusive definition of the vocation of a minister of the Word. Who could sum up the meaning of his manifold activity in the pulpit and the confessional, in teaching and interviews, in conversation with the godly and the ungodly, in dealing with those he fears and those who fear him? Every attempted definition would have to include clear indications that he is called to be a man of prayer. Part of his preparation for prayer is made through the care he gives to the exercise of his ministry and that ministry can only begin in prayer and should end in prayer. The study of the ministry of the Word is a devotional study for the preacher; his work on the construction of sentences, his shaping of paragraphs, his experiments with rhythms and images can all of them be spiritual exercises.

CHAPTER TWO

PREACHER AND POET—AN ANALOGY

IT is often said in criticism 'And here the analogy breaks down', showing that the analogy has been arbitrarily treated as an allegory. The authentic criticism of an analogy concerns its precision and here precision does not mean an exact parallel (a preacher is not exactly like a poet) but the nearest approximation that can be made. When the creature, consciously or unconsciously, denies his creatureliness and claims knowledge that only his Creator has, he is apt to make statements intended to be taken literally where no such statements can be made, and he is prone to use analogies as allegories. This denial of creatureliness is so common to sinful man that those who use analogies must be watchful, hoping that they may be quick to perceive any tendency to treat them as definitions or allegories. An analogy gives one main indication of the nature of its subject, and in doing so certain lesser indications may be given. The parable of the importunate widow is an analogy about prayer; begin to treat the parable allegorically and the difference between an analogy and an allegory becomes plain and it will also become clear that one cannot turn an analogy into an allegory because it suits one's purpose to do so. The tendency to allegorize is the result of assuming both an exactness of knowledge which is not creaturely and a similarity between the objects of attention which does not exist in the real world where contrasts are as apparent as comparisons.

Every significant utterance is a wound, but 'faithful are the wounds of a friend'. Great poets and preachers are known by their compassion as well as for their penetration. They move men not by clumsy attack but by an utterance at once subtle and precise. '. . . expanded explanation tends to spoil the lion's leap. . . . The lion's leap would be mitigated to harmlessness if the lion were

clawless, so precision is both impact and exactitude.'[1] Ezra Pound
has a great deal to say to poets about the precision which makes the
leap effective. Ministers of the Word might well consider what he
has to say. Here is some of his advice in his own words.

> 'There is to be direct treatment of the "thing" whether
> subjective or objective.
> . . . Use absolutely no word that does not contribute to the
> presentation.
> The more concretely and vividly we express the interaction
> of things the better the poetry. . . . We cannot exhibit the
> wealth of nature by mere summation, by piling of sentences.
> Poetic thought works by suggestion, crowding maximum
> meaning into the single phrase, pregnant, charged, and
> luminous from within.
> Poetry must be as well written as prose. Its language must be
> fine language, departing in no way from speech save by a
> heightened intensity (i.e. simplicity). There must be no book
> words, no periphrases, no inversions. . . . There must be no
> interjections. No flying off to nothing. Granted we can't get
> perfection every shot this must be our intention.
> There must be no clichés, set phrases, stereotyped jour-
> nalese. . . .
> Language is made of concrete things. General expressions,
> non-concrete terms, are a laziness; they are not art, not
> creation. . . .
> The only adjective that is worth using is the adjective that
> is essential to the sense of the passage and not the decorative
> frill adjective.
> Every literary sin, every book word, fritters a scrap of the
> reader's patience, a scrap of your sincerity.'[2]

It is never enough to know how to talk unless the speaker has
something to say, but he must never abandon the study of technique, for the man who neglects the science of his profession is
soon at the end of his resources.

[1] Marianne Moore, *Predilections*, Faber & Faber, 1956, pp. 3-4.
[2] Ezra Pound, letters quoted by Herbert Read, *The True Voice of
Feeling*, Faber & Faber, 1953, p. 123, pp. 125-6.

The Gospel is first and foremost something that is told, so a sermon can be described primarily as the attempt made by a preacher to tell something to a group of people on a particular occasion. His style is not a matter of taste or an accomplishment which he can learn; it grows out of his increasing awareness of himself as a being who lives in two worlds. He is not to be a slave in either world; only the free can speak the truth and only the truth makes men free. The value of his constant efforts to speak the truth depends on his study of those he addresses, his attempt to understand his limitations while using his abilities to the full, and on his continual attention to the subject of his utterances. The truth of the Gospel cannot be expressed in set formulae but only in authentic forms which are characteristic of the style of the preacher—and the style of the preacher must be characteristic of the man.

What Sir Herbert Read says about modern poetry could also be said about preaching: '. . . what is specially modern about our poetry is not form as such, but rather a realization that form is the natural effect of the poet's integrity. . . . I begin, therefore, by assuming a radical distinction between the rhetorical form of poetry and what I call the natural or organic form of poetry: and I believe that it was not merely a new phase of literature that began the Romantic movement in Europe, but a new and immensely more vital and interesting conception of literature itself. Poetry ceased to be a game; it began to be a mode of apprehension, an effort of consciousness. We may regret that sonnets, like wigs, have gone out of fashion, and if worn as fancy dress only serve to disguise our feelings. The ideal is now, both in clothes and poetry, to dress as inconspicuously as possible.'[1] Form is the natural effect of the preacher's integrity . . . the ideal is now, both in preaching and in poetry, to dress as inconspicuously as possible, but the dress must be appropriate both for the subject and those who are likely to give attention. 'Voltaire objected to those who said in

[1] Herbert Read, *The True Voice of Feeling*, Faber & Faber, 1953, pp. 9-10.

THE MINISTRY OF THE WORD

enigmas what others said naturally, and we agree; yet we must have the courage of our pecularities.'[1] We can only speak according to our maturity at the time of our utterance; gaucherie is to be pre-ferred to borrowed fluency. Coleridge said that poetry was the best thoughts in the best words, and so is preaching. Those who preach must have a feeling for words, a respect for their worth and a regard for their limitations, remembering always that the context both illuminates and is illuminated by the separate words that make it. Our work, therefore, is fundamentally concerned with the form of a sermon rather than with separate sentences and words. Words have no private lives but their individuality is apparent:

> . . . where every word is at home,
> Taking its place to support the others,
> The word neither diffident nor ostentatious,
> An easy commerce with the old and new,
> The common word exact without vulgarity,
> The formal word precise but not pedantic,
> The complete consort dancing together.[2]

Words are neither to be our slaves nor our masters; they are to be our friends, we are to be at ease with them, dependent on none of them, living a life more than a little beyond their reach.

' "Mere technical display", as Plato says, "is a beastly noise. . . ." '[3] The technique is not all-important, neither is the poetry or the preaching. That an attempt is made to speak the truth is of more importance than the immediate form of its expression, 'For last year's words belong to last year's language.'[4] Idioms flower and decay with the season, but the truth which they served remains. In a sense, as T. S. Eliot shows, the poetry does not matter, and neither does the sermon; what matters is the

---

[1] Marianne Moore, *Predilections*, Faber & Faber, 1956, p. 6.
[2] T. S. Eliot, *Four Quartets*, Faber & Faber, 1944, pp. 42-3.
[3] Marianne Moore, *Predilections*, Faber & Faber, 1956, p. 6.
[4] T. S. Eliot, *Four Quartets*, Faber & Faber, 1944, p. 39.

ineffable thing that preacher or poet attempts to say. Though the poet knows that ultimately the poetry does not matter it is of more account than anything else at the moment of writing and cannot be written where there is insufficient mastery of technique to keep the verse free from self-consciousness. Great poetry in revealing its subject conceals much of the poet yet manifests his most profound experiences through the meaningfulness that moves in and out of the rhythm of words and succession of images. 'The poetry does not matter.'[1] In a sense the sermon does not matter, what matters is what the preacher cannot say because the ineffable remains the ineffable and all that can be done is to make gestures towards it with the finest words that can be used. David danced before the Lord, and Michal despised him in her heart for his abandon. The preacher's use of words is his dance before the Lord; the thoughtless may consider his abandon undisciplined, but his abandon is the fruit of habitual discipline begun in faith and continued in the reason that faith nourishes and by which he protects himself from folly and falsehood. He must study words and forms, he must consider images and rhythm in case he should say what he neither means nor wishes to say. Much of his work is like that of the poet, and like the poet he only achieves spontaneity after much labour; not that labour is the cause of spontaneity, but it makes the condition in which spontaneity can be given him. Poets and preachers are moved whenever they remember that forms of words are expressions of the ceaseless creative activity of God without whom no words can be made and used in meaningful conjunction. When a preacher releases his fellows from sightlessness and narrowness he is making a practical expression of his love of God and of his fellows which art makes possible. On account of this power of art some hold that it can be a substitute for or superior to religion, but where religion is weak art is insipid or exhibitionist, and religion declines if it neglects to use art. A preacher without the poet's approach to life and language could never be precise.

[1] T. S. Eliot, *The Four Quartets*, Faber & Faber, 1944, p. 17.

To talk of the meaning of a poem or a sermon is evidence of an attitude about poems and sermons that needs some thought. Poetry and preaching are rightly spoken of as means of communication and are often approved or disapproved of in so far as their communication is judged to be direct and plain. But is the meaning of a poem or sermon capable of being put in one single sentence? To what one unambiguous sentence could a Christmas sermon be reduced? Can one speak truly of the incarnation without reference to the whole body of Christian doctrine? If all that a sermon or a poem said could be put in one sentence, would there be any point in making sermons or poems? No brief summary can be made of the Sermon on the Mount; its totality offers no exact definition of discipleship, it is a manifestation of the countless ways a man should feel and think about discipleship and practise it. The Sermon on the Mount has economy of words, it has the unity of sublime coherency, it is at once a perfect sermon and a perfect poem.

I. A. Richards says: 'Communication . . . takes place when one mind so acts upon its environment that another mind is influenced, and in that other mind an experience occurs which is like the experience in the first mind, and is caused in part by that experience.'[1] But what of the experience of the first mind? Wordsworth said that poetry is emotion recollected in tranquillity, and some might say that of preaching too. But there is no tape recorder in the mind by which the record of a former experience can be played back at the will of the individual. To recall an experience is a new experience which transforms what is recalled; recalling an experience therefore cannot be an exact reproduction of what happened. The recalling is a new experience in its own right and the expression of what is recalled is a further distinct experience. 'Communication takes place when one mind so acts upon its environment that another mind is influenced . . .' The foregoing reflection on experience is an attempt to put into words what Richards

[1] I. A. Richards, *Principles of Literary Criticism*, Kegan Paul, Trench Trubner, 1938, p. 177.

seems to mean when he talks of a mind acting upon its environment and consequently it is also an attempt towards a description of the creative act of making sermons or poetry. A sermon or a poem is never a reproduction; it is always a new creation. To repeat a former sermon is to make a new one even if a full manuscript is used. The preacher changes between sermon and sermon and at the time of the preaching the personnel of the congregation has a subtle effect upon him changing him still more. The nuances of an altered emphasis as he reads his full manuscript could make him aware of the differences within himself since the first preaching of the sermon.

A poem and a sermon both provide points where past and future meet in the fleeting brevity of the present; each is a sudden illumination of human experience. To put it in another way, each makes an atmosphere in which there can be a heightened awareness of experience and a clearer realization of its significance. Unlike an advertisement, a poem or a sermon does not try to impose something on those who pay attention. Poets and preachers cannot predict or control the response that people make to their utterances; to make a poem or a sermon is to give it a life of its own. T. S. Eliot says, 'The poem's existence is somewhere between the writer and the reader; it has a reality which is not simply the reality of what the writer is trying to express. . . .'[1] This could well be said of a sermon if an alteration in the words quoted is not presumptuous. The sermon's existence is somewhere between the preacher and the members of the congregation; it has a reality which is not simply the reality of what the preacher is trying to express.

Poems and sermons depend on words, but mere examination of the words used does not reveal the secret of the poem's life or the sermon's life. In B. P. Blackmur's way of thinking, the secret lies in the gesture made with the words. He says, 'The great part of our knowledge of life and of nature . . . comes to us as gesture,

---

[1] T. S. Eliot, *The Use of Poetry and the Use of Criticism*, Faber & Faber, 1933, p. 30.

and we are masters of the skill of that knowledge before we can ever make a rhyme or a pun, or even a simple sentence. Nor can we master language purposefully without re-mastering gesture within it. Gesture, in language, is the outward and dramatic play of inward and imaged meaning. It is that play of meaningfulness among words which cannot be defined in the formula in the dictionary, but which is defined in their use together; gesture is that meaningfulness which is moving, in every sense of the word: what moves the words and what moves us.'[1] Following Blackmur's thought, the preacher's task is to look for the language with which to make intelligible gesture to the men of his generation, and he might well apply the following advice to himself: '. . . there are times . . . when the task is to catch up with the changes in colloquial speech, which are fundamentally changes in thought and sensibility. . . . I do not believe that the task of the poet is primarily and always to effect a revolution in language. It would not be desirable, even if it were possible, to live in a state of perpetual revolution: the craving for continual novelty in language . . . is as unwholesome as the obstinate adherence to the idiom of our grandfathers.'[2] 'Art', says de Burgh, 'is able to call into clear expression the dim background of human consciousness in contact with the dim background of reality.'[3] In the pulpit art loses that power if there is a 'craving for novelty' or 'obstinate adherence to the idiom of our grandfathers'.

The preacher is ultimately known for something other than skill with words. It is his holding fast to sound doctrine that makes his skill with words possible and the patterns he weaves with them meaningful; what he does when he is not making sermons gives his sermons life. He is to remember that all genuine work has genuine results: from time to time his blunt sentences will reverberate with the ineffable and his lips will proclaim things

[1] B. P. Blackmur, *Language as Gesture*, George Allen & Unwin, 1954, p. 6.

[2] T. S. Eliot, *Selected Prose*, edited by John Hayward, Penguin Books, 1953, p. 63.

[3] W. G. de Burgh, *The Life of Reason*, Macdonald & Evans, 1949, p. 77.

more tremendous than he knows. The preacher waits for such moments in faith, but with no post-dated hope, for charity which delivers faith from vagueness also saves hope from becoming presumption.

Perhaps all who write great poetry are carried into the realms of religion whether they know it or not, but it is certainly true that the attempt to express religious truths carries a man into the realms of poetry whether he knows it or not. B. P. Blackmur quotes one of the masters of both religion and poetry in the following passage: 'Poetry is the meaning of meaning, or at least the prophecy of it. "Behold all ye that kindle a fire, that compass yourselves about with sparks: walk in the light of your fire, and in the sparks that ye have kindled." In these words of Isaiah there is a motto for poetry, a judgment of poetry, and a poetic gesture which carries the prophetic meaning of poetry. The words sound with music, make images which are visual, seem solid like architecture, repeat themselves like the movements of a dance, call for a kind of mummery in the voice when read, and turn on themselves like nothing but the written word. Yet it is the fury in the words which we understand, and not the words themselves.'[1] What is a motto for poetry could also be one for preaching.

[1] B. P. Blackmur, *Language as Gesture*, George Allen & Unwin, 1954, p. 12.

CHAPTER THREE

AUTHORITY

ALL artists and ministers of the Word must frequently satisfy themselves that they can answer questions in justification of their use of time and energy. They will be asked: Why this style of life? What good does your work do? Why this attempt to communicate what seems incommunicable through words that few understand and by deeds that are bewildering? By what authority do you do these things? Is there any authority in life other than personal whim? Or is it that we are conditioned by impersonal social forces? No creative worker can achieve much unless this sort of question ceases to disturb him because he is as certain as a man can be that what he is doing is significant. Men crave to be absolutely certain that what they do is significant, bearing the clear marks of its significance within it. But only God can so act; it is divine to know certainty and human to know uncertainty. Christian faith does not deliver a man from uncertainty and a longing for demonstrable evidence of authority. The fact that the service of God is perfect freedom provokes the question: Is this particular service authentic? The authority which justifies a man's work is expressed in the work itself. An authoritative statement is not so merely because of the occasion or personality of the speaker; it is authoritative in that he is a divine agent. Thus finite beings are given moments of greatness, the mortal puts on immortality, the corruptible tongue speaks incorruptible things. When ministers of the Word are not speaking or preparing to speak they frequently turn their minds to the subject of authority; in so doing they are helped to speak boldly as they ought to speak in full assurance of the dominical pronouncement: 'He that receiveth you receiveth me, and he that receiveth me receiveth him that sent me.'

Our Lord 'in the same night that he was betrayed, took bread;

and, when he had given thanks, he brake it, and gave it to his disciples, saying, Take, eat, this is my body which is given for you . . .' That night there was that which he could only do by the use of words and that which he could only do through deeds. Every word of his had power and every deed significance; his words and deeds alike communicated truth and needed neither qualification nor commendation. Part of the mystery of that last night consists in that he could not have done what he did without the company of his disciples. He broke them from the ties of family, work and village community and welded them into a body, a means of his expression of himself in the world and to the world. Directly they began to be with him something of his glory and authority rested on them, strengthening and illuminating them.

The Gospel is always proclaimed by words and deeds and never without the common life of a group. It is about the present, proclaimed by men of the present to men of the present; its modernity is one of the marks of its authority. Every proclamation of the Gospel is a powerful act and the power of the act can never be adequately considered in rational terms alone, but a minister of the Word abandons reason at his peril when someone asks him about the authority and power of the Gospel. Ministers of the Word live and preach in an age when there is general perplexity and bewilderment about authority; the language and thought of the pulpit frequently show this both directly and indirectly. Some would have religion as a necessity to provide the authoritative basis on which constructive thought could be rested. But foundation and superstructure are a unity interdependent and affecting one another after the manner of the parts of a living entity. No foundation will hold stubble or hay in place or turn dross into gold—faith and magic have always to be carefully distinguished no matter how intellectually or appealingly magic may be dressed. In an age of revolution in thought many are disturbed by the place of unprovable assumptions in life and in consequence are doubtful whether there can be any knowledge of reality. A modern poet says:

All that I love is, like the night, outside,
Good to be gazed at, looking as if it could
With a simple gesture be brought inside my head
Or in my heart. But my thoughts about it divide
Me from my object. Now deep in my bed
I turn and the world turns on the other side.[1]

Christian faith does not smooth out the difficulties of mental life but it makes them bearable and provides a means whereby men can establish enough order and law over the chaos of thinking and feeling to make significant living possible. At this point in history all are upset, consciously and unconsciously, by the fact that all thinking rests on axioms; many actively suffer through fancying that they are faced with near insanity if the search for the provable to take the place of the axiomatic finally fails. This is the temper which manifests itself in the common question which is not 'Can I believe in God?' but 'Can I believe in belief?' The minister of the Word does not set out to help men by argument but by making as clear authoritative statements as he can. He is to affirm what Christianity has always known, namely, that there are valid and necessary mental processes other than discursive reasoning—which has an essential place but always a subordinate one—for what use would reasoning be if there were nothing to reason about? Perception brings the object into the mind and reason apprehends it, but there can only be perception where something is given. This leads the minister of the Word to the specific religious statement that all mental life begins in God who is the maker of thought as he is the maker of the objects of thought. The serious person who cannot accept this statement as true must be helped to make clear to himself the grounds on which he rejects it. Irreligious and religious people alike are vexed by the questions they ask about the nature of authority and the means by which it may be recognized, and are more disturbed if they suppress these questions.

In poetry, literature, drama and painting there are plain

[1] Elizabeth Jennings, 'In the Night' from *Collected Poems*, Macmillan & Co., 1967.

manifestations of the predicament characteristic of our day, the predicament of men who ask questions about life and death, about love and hate, about the meaning of speech and the reality of thought; they can no more than set about answering these questions and in consequence there are some who are uneasy or derisive when the Church seems to them to pretend to an exactness of knowledge not vouchsafed to finite minds and beyond the powers of finite minds to attain. Many serious people are impressed by the single-mindedness of artists and by the fact that the artists' attempts to discuss matters of ultimate human concern seem more real and potentially understandable than the theologians' wrestling to get the better of ecclesiastical idioms. Some Christians have the naïve idea that the arts, specially drama, could and should be extensively used for the proclamation of the Gospel. In the first place Christian artists cannot easily and quickly find a way of expressing Christian doctrine in a community which is not moved by Christian symbols. Indeed at present there is no common symbolism, Christian or otherwise, and Christian artists are found incomprehensible and disturbing by their fellow-Christians who cannot justify the authority of new forms and somehow feel that old forms might be patched and brought up-to-date. In the second place whenever the Church tries to use art as a method of propaganda her integrity and authority are severely questioned by just those whose conversion would be most significant. The Church has a duty to safeguard the arts as genuine human activities good in their own right, providing valid ways for thinking truth and expressing it. It is possible to tell lies with paint and canvas or in melody; it is possible for artists to tell lies through imperfect mastery of technique or through ignorance of the limitations of the medium of expression used. 'My lord, the strings are false'—this may be so, though more often the falsity is in the musician; but when he is single-minded, he tends, like all other serious artists today, to be accepted as one who speaks with authority. Christians, and particularly ministers of the Word, should recognize this authority within its own sphere. Authority can recognize authority (see Matt. 8.9); it all has the same source and no man can have any if it is not given him.

To think about authority is to think at the same time about revelation, faith and freedom. Authority is not the static manifestation of power at one particular point in time giving unquestionable directions to all generations. Authority is the name for an element in a living relationship and consequently eludes exact definition. We can look at the question in this way: we respect those we love; this respect is one of the ingredients of love, part of the movement and expression of love. In human affection there is this recognizable exercise of both authority and submission within relationships which only comes to light when affection is endangered and its state made obvious in the protests: 'What right had he to expect that of me?', 'I made up my mind that I would not give in again.' Where affection is strong, bearing none of the burdens of misunderstanding, there is no attempt to analyse respect as a separate entity because it is treated as belonging to the love that genders and is engendered by it. Friends respect one another, they give one another authority and they obey one another. This authority and this obedience are not absolute but reflections of the authority and obedience within the relationship which includes all relationships—the relationship of God and man where God delegates authority to men as a friend would to friends. That there can be denial of or rebellion against absolute authority is not a defect in its nature nor are its claims lessened thereby. These claims are made in love and so seem weak and uncertain, but the strength of divine love is always in the weakness that we recall in remembering the crown of thorns, the soldier's cloak and the criminal's cross. Absolute authority is not a thing and it cannot be considered apart from its manifestations and from the obedience it calls forth. To talk about authority and obedience when we speak of the love of God is not to talk about discernible and distinct entities, but however unsatisfactory the concepts of authority and obedience may be in this connexion we must still use them as approximate descriptions of experience.

God's authority has to be revealed before it can be apprehended, and the apprehension is of faith and must be freely made. Ministers of the Word cannot use open violence or subtle coercion to compel people to submit to the authority of God. Ministers of the Word are not powerless, for they have authority, a unique authority which can only be uniquely wielded. Paley gives advice to young preachers to the effect that they should be neither too vague nor yet too exact. The authority of the minister of the Word is manifest in his leaving only partly described what can only be partly described, no matter how disappointed or distressed his hearers may be. Every authentic proclamation of the Gospel has always a definite indefiniteness about it. The statement that rings with finality is false, it lacks the audacity of truthfulness which intentionally leaves rough edges. Statements about the nature of authority are not frequently made in the pulpit but the preacher is always to speak with authority and his most authoritative utterances are made when the Word most clearly resounds in his words. His efforts alone do not bring this about yet it cannot happen without his constant work. Ministers of the Word think about authority in solitude, they discuss it in the proper company, but for the greater part of their life they are not called to talk about authority but to speak and act with authority. What we think about our authority and how we think about it determines our use of it on the manifold occasions of our ministry.

The authority of God is unique, hence the authority of the Church is unique and can only be affirmed uniquely. The authority of the Church looks weak and is hidden by the sinfulness of its members who often turn aside from their most serious occupations for the most trivial reasons. It is not its members that make the Church, it is the Church that makes its members; but we do not believe in God because we believe in the Church, we believe in the Church because we believe in God. In the name of God we state but we do not dictate; we dare not entice, but what we say is to be said in profound confidence and certainty despite its seeming indefiniteness. We do not make a simple authoritarian demand for submission to the direction of an infallible Body, or an infallible book or formula; we do not demand that people should accept the literal interpretation of the Scriptures or a mechanical explanation of the sacraments. Directly we say that authority is completely expressed in the Bible, we rob the Body and the sacraments of their proper significance and throw doubt on the value of the Bible's witness to their authenticity. If we say that authority rests in the autonomous life of the Body, which preceded the Bible in time, we undermine the importance of Scripture and sacraments and encourage some type of gnosticism. If we centre authority in the operation of the sacraments we do away with the safeguards which prevent them from being regarded with superstition or suspicion, for of course sacraments depend on the authenticity of the life of the Body ever expressing itself in new ways and never denying its origin and destiny as described in Scripture. All attempts to localize authority, saying that it lies here or that it lies there, end in confusion. Denial of any of the particular manifestations of authority at once throws doubt on all of its manifestations. It cannot be said that authority resides in the common will of church members or in the maintenance of a certain doctrine of the ministry, yet an irregular ministry would falsify authority and an absence of common will would maim its expression.

In speaking and thinking of authority it is probably better to personify it than to think of it as a thing to be fixed in time and place or a power that is capable of being used by individuals or groups. To personify authority attaches to it the mystery and elusiveness that pertains to the highest kind of life we know and indicates an autonomy that we cannot control because it is an expression of the life of God whose every revelation is authoritative. To use an analogy from art, a picture is the painter's authoritative statement; the authority is not in the picture's colour, its form or its texture, nor is it in them taken all together, yet its authority cannot be expressed without them. God reveals himself continually but never completely in the common life of the

Church, in its Scriptures, in its sacraments, in the functions of its ministers. Wherever he reveals himself, there is the manifestation of his authority, for every deed of his contains within it its justification, but not the kind of justification that finite men can fully apprehend. So ministers of the Word are left to rejoice in partial knowledge and wield the authority that is delegated to them. 'Now we know in part and we prophesy in part.' Our knowledge is fragmentary, but it is real knowledge; our best speech is broken speech, but it is significant speech. Our authority as ministers is not our own, it is given us—it makes us what we are, we do not make it what it is, though indiscreet explanations give impressions to the contrary.

Faith is not the absence of doubt and uncertainty, but the bearing of both in an attempt to answer questions which cannot be completely answered. Faith does not silence questions about authority but sharpens them: By what authority is it said that sacraments are effectual, that the use we make of the Bible is authentic? By what authority is it stated that the Church is a divine agent in the world? By what authority do we deny or affirm the limits of the individual's right of private judgment? Authority is in an area to which we are led by every attempt to justify sacraments, Scriptures, Church and the reality of individual religious experience. In that area we know ceaseless movement and in the movement we realize again and again that authority and revelation cannot be separated—what we believe about the mode of revelation we also believe about authority's mode of expression. Every question about authority is always a question about revelation and revelation cannot be talked about clearly because it is the light by which we see.

The minister of the Word's questions about authority are perennial and he must set about answering them if he is to be eloquent on useful matters. He must think and live in his own age and not exist vicariously, by way of text-books, in an epoch long since or lately gone; even the issues of ten years ago are now very much past and so are the corresponding idioms of thought and speech. At this point in the century Christian and non-Christian, theologian and philosopher, scientist and artist, share a common unease in an increasingly clear sight of the ramifications consequent upon the realization of the inexactness and incompleteness of all human knowledge. As a result men doubt the reliability of imagination, reasoning and memory, and many fancy themselves lost in a shipwreck of the mind having discovered the limitations of syllogistic thought and the true nature of what they considered to be the exact sciences. Wise ministers of the Word do not rejoice naïvely in this as a real opportunity for immediate evangelism, for the breakdown of confidence in mental processes and the emergence of a new way of life gives them the responsibility of finding the new forms of speech and the new pattern of Christian behaviour through which the truth of the Gospel may bring light and freedom into the disorder of our day.

This generation seeks a sign. We can only offer the sign of the inconclusive conclusion, that is the conclusion which has the seeds of conclusiveness within it. We dare not pretend that harvest and spring come together, nor can we deny that sowing and reaping are both laborious and that a man's endurance is tested by the interval between. What ministers of the Word say may seem too little to live on, but they must not go beyond their authority in a mistaken attempt to make their authority strong and clear. That going beyond is always the outcome of an atheistic anxiety, or a sign that the man of God has succumbed to the temptation to speak as a god, to come in his own name and to be his own authority.

CHAPTER FOUR

THE EXPOSITION OF DOCTRINE

SIMPLE people recognize the complexity of life without resentment. They think, mindful that their thinking must do justice to this complexity, and they attempt to speak to others in language that neither minimizes nor overestimates the extent of human knowledge. Simplicity of speech is most nearly achieved in the frank acceptance of the mystery of reality and of the mysterious nature of words as parts of the reality they are used to describe. Added to this the speaker must constantly remember that he is part of the reality he discusses; in fact when he speaks of anything he is inevitably talking about himself, for he is not a spectator of the complexity of life but a factor in it, because he partly makes the complexity he seeks to understand. Religion is not a way of mastering this complexity but of bearing it. Christian doctrine does not offer a complete interpretation of human experience but suggests a way towards its interpretation, nor does Christian doctrine claim that examination of human experience will provide a final satisfactory way of checking the truths of the Christian revelation. But where there can be no exact disclosure of the meaningfulness of human experience or literal statement of doctrine it is nevertheless possible to talk significantly about each in terms of the other. For instance, it is not given to a minister of the Word to state the exact meaning of the corporate experiences shared by members of the body of Christ, yet he can say a great deal that is pertinent about church membership.

Ministers of the Word are always being led to reflect on the nature of Christian doctrine as well as on its content in their work to achieve the coherency necessary for intelligible speech in the pulpit, in the confessional and on all the manifold occasions of their ministry. To proclaim sound doctrine means that it must be firmly held through the ups and downs of moods, in disasters, in disappointments, in achievements and in triumphs. The way to hold it is largely found through reflections on its nature and its content. There is an old saying that the monk who knows he is praying is not praying. It could be said that a minister of the Word who is consciously aware of himself as doctrinally sound is not doctrinally sound. Doctrinal soundness would be to think the truth and do the truth and pray the truth in that full state of self-affirmation which is that self-forgetfulness which no direct conscious efforts can create. That is the aim; to know it is not the same as having achieved it, to travel is not to arrive but in the journeying we are vouchsafed some knowledge of our journey's end. This chapter suggests the sort of reflections which might be made by a minister of the Word in the hope that it will be given him to speak boldly as he ought to speak.

If Christian doctrine were the formulation of a complete knowledge of reality or if it presented the principle of interpretation through which every experience could be completely explained, then the holding of doctrine would be determined accordingly, and so would its exposition. But Christian doctrine does not claim to tell exactly why and exactly how God creates; it does not claim to tell exactly why and exactly how God became man without ceasing to be God. Christian doctrine does not offer a full explanation of the birth, life, death, resurrection and ascension of the Lord whereby we are saved from the bondage of sin and death and time and the order of this world. It does not offer a man the definition of his identity or of what constitutes his differences from and likenesses to all other human beings. Christian doctrine does not enable a man to see the reason for earthquake, tornado, typhoon, for pain, war, death and treachery. A neat doctrinal system rounded and conclusive could only be built with the support of extra axioms brought in to supplement those that revelation gives. The mind when left to itself plays tricks and scrupulous theologians must be quick to detect the introduction of unwarranted axioms in an attempt to make complete what must be left incomplete. To hold sound doctrine always means the maintenance of a system of thought through which every new fact of experience can be interpreted to the degree that interpretation is possible. A false doctrinal system is one that dismisses awkward experiences as irrelevant or imposes an interpretation which is convenient rather than truthful. A true system safeguards the reality of partial human knowledge and so orders this knowledge that a man may realize that the totality of his experiences makes sense even if he cannot fully see it.

Christian doctrine may be stated in the simplest of words, and is best so stated, but this must never be the occasion for deception by implying that the simplicity of the words does away with the complexity of the subject. 'God is love' is one of the most profound Christian statements that can be made, but Christians who make it have to be ready to answer any who might ask, What do you mean by the word *love*? which of the possible meanings of the word *is* do you intend in your statement? Christians are taught to say that God is our father and the phrase is taught on the highest authority. It is right that we should speak of God as a person, for person is the name of the highest kind of life we know. But by speaking of God as a person we have not made a definition. We do not know fully what we mean by the word *person*; it is the word we use to signify our limited knowledge of what it means to be human. So if anyone uses the statement 'God is a person' as if it were a simple equation he must remember that he is dealing with two partially unknowns, and if he gets over this difficulty by selecting a definition of *person*, then he gets no more out of the equation than he has put into it. Whatever he does he cannot prove his answer, for God continues to be not fully knowable. Nevertheless the most significant deductions in the world are made from the statement that God is a person and in making them theologians learn that to be mature is to be dogmatic where it is right to be dogmatic and agnostic where it is proper to be agnostic. To be a Christian is not to be delivered out of finite limitations but to see them clearly and to know the vastness of the resources within them and the richness of thought and life that belongs to human beings. Grace does not lift us out of nature; it makes all nature ours in the movement of our transcending it. But finite man is also sinful man, and all are prone to fall into the way of thinking the thoughts they choose to think, regardless of the nature of the subject of their thinking, thus coming to exact conclusions, whereas Christian doctrine continually asserts the finiteness of human beings whose redemption does not deliver them from their creaturely limitations.

Fear of error is the greatest enemy of truth. The minister of the Word needs to be fearless in his thinking if he is to be truthful and humble in his speaking. Ministers of the Word sometimes encourage one another to dread error rather than reverence truth. Those who dread error talk in a pattern of qualified statements where each qualifying statement drains the meaning out of the statement it qualifies. Fear of error also leads to such carefully balanced utterances that the force of a sermon is lost in an array of citations from theologians who are given opposing positions and seem to struggle against one another on the fringes of the sermon, and the struggle is gradually brought into such a position of prominence that the rest of the sermon is hidden. Sometimes a sermon is spoiled by unresolved conflicts in the preacher's mind which show themselves by broken sentences, by paragraphs unfinished or artificially finished and by excessive speed over unmade roads in the course of the sermon's journey. Christian doctrine is not given that we may avoid mistakes in our thought and utterance. Christian doctrine is given so that we can think and talk positively in full recognition that no minister of the Word is the sole agent, that his is not the only sermon that people listening will ever have the opportunity to hear. To think positively is to discover that the minister of the Word's true doctrinal position is always on the fringes of error. We can only think our clearest thoughts and speak our most authoritative words from the frontiers of error; for example, our clearest statements of the omnipotence of God almost deny the freedom of man. But there is a more apt metaphor from modern warfare where battles are fought in zones rather than from behind fixed lines; mental operations are better considered as the movement and counter-movement of thoughts and feelings in zones, and the thing is to control the movement not by restricting its range but by paying attention to its purpose; thus he who moves freely in the zones will have eloquence. Eloquence is the art of putting into words that which is extremely difficult to put into words. It is the minister of the Word's vocation to be eloquent in this sense. That eloquence cannot be without the adventure of holding doctrine in such a way that one is always in danger of losing one's grip of it. Our religion rests on the foundation of theism which can only be made real to the mind by continual meditation on the doctrine of creation, which puts one in danger of pantheism and a denial of the necessity of the Incarnation. It is only by reflection on the creative activity of God that the full glory of the Incarnation can be seen, for when every creative act is recognized as an act of revelation then it can be seen how the one act that is the revelation of revelations illuminates and is illuminated by all other acts of God. It is only by thinking emphatically about the humanity of our Lord that one can realize his divinity, while it is only by concentrated reflection on his divinity that the reality of his manhood is apprehended. In other words, meditation on his being must always be concerned both with his earthly ministry and his eternal sovereignty, because meditation is not part of a process that ends in a finished conclusion, it is the prelude to adoration of the mystery that is God. All theology begins in adoration and ends in adoration, but it can only end in adoration if emotion, imagination, intelligence are not stifled but used by the preacher in the pursuit of his calling, which may be described as an attempt to master words sufficiently to expound the truth which in mastering men frees them from the errors born in sin and from the errors that give birth to sins. And at this point one is led to remember that it is only by considering the power of God's grace that one begins to understand the nature of the human effort required in individual man's salvation; it is only by seriously considering the nature of this human effort that one begins to know the ceaseless activity of God in which all human action has its beginning. It is by devotion to Christ in the Blessed Sacrament that one discovers most fully that where the Word is not spoken the bread will not be broken. It is only through diligent attention to the necessity for the spoken word that the essential nature of the sacraments is realized—where the bread is not broken soon the Word will not be spoken. The importance of the ministry is most clearly seen when one is at the point of denying it; the significance of the Church's corporate life can best be seen at the point where one is about to deny it in emphasizing the value of the individual; the value of each individual is most clearly seen when one is about to deny it in affirming the value of the corporate. A truth is often capable of being most clearly seen when it is about to be denied.

The minister of the Word does his clearest thinking on the edges of error, he is most orthodox when on the point of coming to heretical conclusions. In a sense thinking means submitting to the movement of the mind, not blindly or mechanically but maintaining a remote control over the movement. This remote control is maintained by the Christian through constant reflection on the limits of his creatureliness in the light of his doctrine. The image for thinking is not movement within a square marked by firm thick lines but rather that of movement in a space bounded by distant but discernible boundaries. Doctrine is not held by supression of thoughts that challenge its truth but by their proper development. Thoughts are not isolated happenings, nor are they like things that can be picked up and thrown away. Each thought is a movement within the movement of the whole mind, and enriches the mind as long as the movement of the mind remains under the remote control of the thinker. The mind is never static: it is always active, often in turmoil, sometimes almost stagnant but never motionless, and no Christian doctrine indicates that a man can completely master his mind by his own efforts; each can understand what these lines signify:

I said to my soul, be still, and wait without hope
For hope would be hope for the wrong thing: there is yet
    faith
But the faith and the love and the hope are all in the waiting.
Wait without thought, for you are not ready for thought:
So the darkness shall be the light, and the stillness the
    dancing.[1]

The stillness is not made by immobility but by the rhythmic movements of a mind that waits in the dark: the waiting becomes the dance and the darkness the light. Ultimately doctrine can only be held by the movement of the whole mind in prayer, where prayer is understood as a habitual state with characteristic activities. The man of prayer, like every creative worker, holds all his powers in tension till he is 'ready for thought'. This is the poise, the active stillness of the creative mind, which no one can maintain indefinitely; from time to time the poise is lost, the stillness is gone and chaos reigns. Again and again order and law must be established, poise recovered and stillness remade. All speech that moves men was minted when some man's mind was poised and still.

To expound doctrine is not to teach a system of thought and then demonstrate that no experience can disturb it. It is not that doctrine is supremely important and that life proves its importance; it is that life is supremely important and doctrine illuminates it. The minister of the Word is called to be an expert in living rather than an expert in doctrine. At the command of the Lord he studies doctrine, he teaches it that people may have life and that they may have it more abundantly. As this chapter is showing, the way doctrine is held shapes the way it is expounded and the way it is held is determined by what a man thinks about its nature and content. Christian doctrine does not provide the answer to every question but the way to begin answering; doctrine does not tell a man what to think but how to think. Revelation is not a huge gift which makes man's work unnecessary and takes away from him all

[1] T. S. Eliot, *Four Quartets*, Faber & Faber, 1944, p. 19.

need of initiative. We are given sufficient knowledge to make the life of faith possible, but to live faithfully does not mean that one is given all knowledge, but rather the ability to live the full human life, being reconciled to and rejoicing in the reality of partial human knowledge. 'He that endures to the end shall be saved': he will have to endure finiteness, he will have to bear the burdens of perplexity and bewilderment, but a man can be steadied for this by all that doctrine shows him about his own nature. He has to be helped to keep in his mind that he is a creature, limited in knowledge and power, that he is a being made in the image of God and capable of relationship with him, that he is a sinner in constant need of forgiveness. These three facts must be kept before his mind at the same time, while he considers the implications of the threefold commandment that is at the centre of our religion, namely, 'Thou shalt love the Lord thy God with all thy heart, with all thy mind and with all thy soul and with all thy strength . . . thou shalt love thy neighbour as thyself.' That is, love God, love your neighbour, love yourself. To love yourself is to think the highest thoughts about yourself, to realize your value as a unique individual and your ability to bring new things into being. The revelation of human greatness is painful when seen in individual terms, it shows the enormity of wasting life on trivialities and the hideousness of the corruption of creative ability which we call sin. The potential goodness of man must be emphasized in such a way that he sees his sinfulness without thinking that he is to regard himself as being unredeemable. There can be no formula for this; the way to attempt it lies both in the minister of the Word's belief about the nature of doctrine and its content and in his understanding of and relationship with the individuals and groups among whom he moves. No one lectures abstractly on doctrine; one talks it to people who are fellow human beings if not also fellow church members; always there is a common tie which makes conversation possible and has much to do with its form. Relationships are living, changing things which make it impossible for any minister of the Word to depend on a few invariable forms for his

use in saying what he has to say. The mental and psychic atmosphere of the day decides the pattern of his secret reflections about
doctrine. The more compassionate a pastor is, the more he is in
danger of speaking heretically, but that danger is inevitable if he is
to discover a way of making himself clear to the men and women
of his generation with that degree of clarity which his subject
permits. But who can be entirely coherent about the whole of life?
That is the size of the preacher's subject, but he can hope that
doctrinal integrity will sharpen the edges of his intelligibility
sufficiently for it to cut through the traffic that blocks the minds of
so many who listen.

Perhaps the most significant consideration of doctrine for the
minister of the Word is that which is concerned with all that the
doctrine of creation implies. This has a direct effect on his whole
conception of preaching and it also enables him to speak in the
pulpit and out of the pulpit in the ways that are most expedient
for this generation. To take the first point: belief in preaching, or
indeed in meaningful conversation, has doctrinal roots or else it
has no roots. To go on believing in the value of human speech and
the possibility of communication can only be justified by what one
believes about the nature of reality. More than that, human speech
is not fully appreciated till it is recognized as a part of creation just
as much as landscapes and shifting clouds. That is, no poem or
sermon comes into being without the divine initiation. A poem or
sermon is made in much the same way as bread is made. Bread
ultimately consists of the energy of the sun, the sustenance given
by rain and soil and the mysterious energy of life within the seeds
sown by men. The loaf on the table is there because God ceaselessly provides all the raw materials necessary including the
psychic energy which enables men to work and co-operate with
one another. The making of bread is a significant human action
which we proclaim every time we reverently place the common
bread on the altar; this common unconsecrated bread is only less
wonderful than the consecrated bread. Before the altar we are
reminded that man does not live by bread alone. He needs the

things that are made by human speech which are nourishment for his mind. Music and the visual arts have their place in life, but whenever speech is absent or deficient the human spirit dwindles and the human mind is bewildered and becomes brutal. The utterances of men are possible because God ceaselessly brings into being the raw materials necessary for their making: we can neither contemplate fulness of human life nor the possibility of our religion bringing that fulness to perfection without the arts, and in particular without the art of ordered speech. It is true that

> The soul of Man must quicken to creation.
> Out of the formless stone, when the artist united himself with stone,
> Spring always new forms of life, from the soul of man that is joined to the soul of stone;
> Out of the meaningless practical shapes of all that is living or lifeless
> Joined with the artist's eye, new life, new form, new colour.
> Out of the sea of sound the life of music,
> Out of the slimy mud of words, out of the sleet and hail of verbal imprecisions,
> Approximate thoughts and feelings, words that have taken the place of thoughts and feelings,
> There spring the perfect order of speech, and the beauty of incantation.[1]

Human speech is never fruitless; they use it best who most frequently ponder its origin and its end.

[1] T. S. Eliot, Choruses from 'The Rock', in *Later Poems, 1925-1935*, Faber & Faber, 1941, pp. 136-7.

CHAPTER FIVE

A NOTE ON THEOLOGICAL 'SCHIZOPHRENIA'

. . . the principal obstacle to true thinking is our desire for justification, the falser an idea the more obvious its justificatory element.[1]

A SCHIZOPHRENIC is not a Jekyll and Hyde personality but a personality so split into isolated fragments that coherent speech and action have died in the death of any single purpose which could be the integrating force of the personality. The schizophrenic is found staring vacantly or talking to himself; he always shows the symptoms of one who is out of touch with reality, living in the fictitious horrors, compensations and terrors which he constructs within himself. This condition can give an analogy for describing the state of a minister of the Word whose theologizing has led him to atomize and distort Christian doctrines. That is, in making the threefold reflection on doctrine, himself as a minister of the Word and those to whom he is to present the Gospel, he makes a false simplification to minimize the difficulties of his work or to construct a hope that is visible to him in immediate concrete terms and capable of quick realization. The following note is a sketch of the early stages of theological 'schizophrenia'; to be brief the word will be used throughout with the limitation of meaning now to be explained.

The term 'schizophrenia' will be used here to indicate the condition of a minister of the Word who holds two contradictory sets of doctrines at the same time, one set being unconsciously held and showing itself through the unspoken assumptions which inform parts of his utterances and make for inconsistencies in his

---

[1] W. H. Auden, *New Year Letter*, Faber & Faber, 1941, p. 132.

pastoral and evangelistic policy. The 'schizophrenic' is seldom more than momentarily aware of his condition; in advanced cases even this momentary awareness seems almost if not completely absent. 'Schizophrenia' is not an intellectual weakness to be treated academically or a failure in common sense to be dealt with by argument. The condition is understood, prevented or treated by methods more to be described as psychological than logical.

Theological discernment is impaired by emotional excesses, and righteous indignation, however controlled, can destroy it. Therefore in considering 'schizophrenia' a certain detachment and objectivity are to be preserved lest those who examine it should become 'schizophrenic' through intense attempts to guard against it in themselves or to cure it in others. Ministers of the Word are to be as wise as serpents and as harmless as doves, that is, they are to be as subtle and patient in their treatment of themselves as they are in their care of others. The enlarging of experience, the need to act and to encourage others to act, the realization that pain has both to be borne and inflicted all combine to make 'schizophrenia' a potential danger for everyone and in particular for those who are called to interpret life in terms of doctrine and doctrine in terms of life.

Some ministers of the Word affirm that the Scriptures are not literally inspired and at the same time they will discuss methods of communicating the Gospel which assume a doctrine of inspiration which is in contradiction to the one they consciously hold about the Scriptures. Such hold that the communication of the Gospel is merely a matter of finding an unequivocal statement while at the same time they are emphatic that the Scriptures are 'not to be taken literally'. These symptoms show a deep-seated 'schizophrenic' condition which is the result of holding consciously that revelation is not given in propositional form and unconsciously that it is given in propositional form. This deep-seated condition is manifested by many who are looking for a group of statements not couched in biblical English but in modern idiom which can be presented as a literal expression of the truth of the Gospel. But where is unambiguous idiom to be found? Some have tried to find images that would serve this purpose and there would be point in an investigation of modern sermon illustrations in this connexion. But is it possible for a minister of the Word to find an image, biblical or otherwise, which would convey exactly what he is determined it should convey, no more and no less? Ultimately the choice of words and the use of images is a doctrinal matter because behaviour is the embodiment of doctrine and the preacher's use of language is an important part of his behaviour. He is called to set men free by presentation of the truth with the freedom that comes from the maintenance of that inner discipline of his thinking which feeds and is fed by the love which bids him be the servant of all rather than attempt to be the master of some.

The desire to have a quick influence over people is one of the seeds of 'schizophrenia'. It leads to the unconscious making of assumptions, as in the following instance. A sermon may begin by an analysis of the present situation based on the doctrine of original sin. This is followed by a rhetorical question: What can we as Christians do? Then a programme of action is outlined and a plea for active participation in the working out of the programme is made with a statement to the effect that the lapsed will respond for they are really good at heart and waiting for a lead or for interest to be shown in them as persons. Indeed it is sometimes stated, after expatiating on the godlessness of modern people in general, that great results would follow if only we had a modern translation of the Bible, a different form of worship, a better spirit in the congregation or more individual Christians showing a good example in office, factory and shop. Thus the sermon's closing exhortation is based on a doctrine of man which is in contradiction to that assumed in the sermon's opening analysis of the situation.

It can happen that a minister of the Word will, in sermon or conversation, speak about the omnipotence of God and the finiteness of the human mind, pointing to the fact that Christians walk by faith and not by sight. He will then go on to make a definite moral judgment on human actions performed in a complicated moral situation as if he had the complete knowledge of the situation which would make such a judgment possible. This urge to make final moral judgments can be the source of 'schizophrenia' or one of the symptoms of it. Many are consciously opposed to being legalistic but in moments of stress assume that approval or disapproval is possible by adherence to the letter of a moral code. This is the dilemma of all who find legalism intolerable and to be without a moral code unbearable. It is of course clear that murder, theft, adultery, perjury are morally indefensible, but there are many human deeds which are not patently classifiable in the half light of human knowledge. 'Schizophrenia' is avoided by bearing the human burden of being content with tentative judgments or with the suspension of judgment in spite of all longings to give unqualified approval or disapproval. Those who resist all claims to be infallible must be in practice what they are in theory; those who claim to be charitable must not be censorious; those who would be truthful must be just, and the just must deal with the facts they know, recognizing that there are unknowable facts in every human situation. This is the position of those who believe that divine guidance does not give man the ability to see and to explain human behaviour in unequivocal terms. Approval is always qualified and disapproval never final. Some people are better unconsciously than they are consciously, for there are those who consciously claim to judge themselves and others ruthlessly by high standards but in concrete particular cases will show the restraint that springs from the justice which is nourished by truth and love—there are 'schizophrenics' who need to preach consciously what they unconsciously practise.

The ministry of the Word is marred by overconcern to be orthodox and effective. The minister's determination to preserve his doctrinal integrity at all costs could be his undoing, for the Word is to be communicated even though the attempt to communicate is dangerous. The constant wish for discernible success leads to a pragmatic approach to preaching which would also be his undoing. Such an approach would keep his utterances within the realms of the familiar and the preaching of the Gospel should always present finite and sinful men and women with much that is strange to their habitual way of feeling and thinking. The pragmatic approach to preaching tempts the preacher to move people by offering a complete explanation where no complete explanation can be given, that is, he is tempted to offer what can only be apprehended by faith as if it were capable of being grasped by reason alone. In his anxiety to encourage Christian action he may lead himself into offering justification for action which contradicts the doctrine of God and man which he states explicitly. Pragmatism can make 'schizophrenics' of us all.

'Schizophrenia' is sometimes manifested by the minister of the Word's silence on useful matters. When this happens the 'schizophrenic' is frequently aware of his condition and regrets his inability to speak with the certainty that is expected in a minister of the Word. He feels himself unable to speak with any clarity on the nature of the divine work and the human effort necessary in salvation; he finds himself unable to say anything significant about the sacraments without denying either God's immanence or transcendence; anything he says about human creative activity leads him into what seems a denial of divine omnipotence; whenever he begins to think of talking about the mystery of evil he discovers that he is beginning to assume that he has sufficient knowledge to justify God. He finds that the sermons on the Passion of our Lord which he begins to make either deny the humanity of our Lord in emphasizing his divinity or deny the divinity of our Lord in emphasizing his humanity. In the same way his thoughts about the reality of the life of this world seem to deny the reality of the life of the world to come and his thoughts about the reality of the world to come leave out of account the reality of the life of this world. When he tries to make plain to himself in what the authority of the Bible lies he finds that he is making it impossible for himself to recognize the authority of the Church; his attempts to make definite the centrality of sacraments in the Christian life make it impossible to give due place to the ministry of the Word without which there could be no sacraments, while his emphasis on the ministry of the Word seems to prevent his giving the sacraments the place he believes to be theirs. All his thought about the disunity of the Church seems to result in either a denial of the efficacy of all sacramental worship outside his own communion, or an assertion that there is no doctrine of the Church. This is a sketch of the causes of the silence of some ministers of the Word on important matters; to break it often means a hardening of the 'schizophrenic' way of life in which the silence has its origin.

Like talents, disorders are deepened by what a man thinks about when he is alone and by how he thinks what he thinks. It matters a good deal whether his habitual method is syllogistic, whether he tends in his private thinking to be inductive or deductive, whether he reasons about courses of action from principles to persons or from persons to principles, whether he is constantly perplexed as to whether faith leads to irrationality or whether reasoning is a process that ultimately makes the life of faith untenable. A man can never decide that when he thinks in solitude he will insulate himself and make himself immune from the psychic forces that operate in the community of which he is a living part. Solitary thinking is largely shaped by the thinker's response to external stimuli, though obviously he has his share in producing the stimuli that are made by communal living. Present conditions stimulate the minister of the Word to prepare himself to speak in terms that will be acceptable to those for whom the idea of faith is absurd, and who feel that reason is the way of life, as well as to those who hold that faith and reason are both illusions. The point is that if the response of the minister of the Word is too violent and hurried there will be disorder with consequent manifestations of 'schizophrenia'. All impetuosity in his thinking is as reprehensible as the torpid movement of mind that marks indifference or despair. Haste to justify the place of the Church in the modern community makes as many difficulties as reluctance or refusal to elucidate the Church's significance. Now as ever, the most searching questions a minister of the Word knows are those which he asks himself. In answering his own questions he must constantly be making clearer his doctrinal position, not justifying it, remembering that he must not underestimate the place of faith to secure the position of reasoning and that he must never exalt reasoning to the detriment of faith. The 'schizophrenic' is the man who tidies up his mind and keeps it tidy: in speech he will tend to be boisterously dogmatic, in the wrong sense of being dogmatic, or he will avoid matters of importance, restricting himself to questions of marginal concern in life, or he will spend nearly all of his sermons exhorting his listeners to pray, to set an example, to know their faith, to accept their civic responsibilities and so on, without any description as to how such things are to be done. As noted earlier, should there be commendation of these exhortations it will be made from a set of doctrinal assumptions unconsciously held and in contradiction of the doctrines to which he consciously adheres.

'Schizophrenia' is avoided by forswearing all false simplifications so as to maintain the essential untidiness of mind consequent on the acceptance of Christian doctrine. This essential untidiness is preserved by habitual refusal to come to definite conclusions where there can be none, without ever denying the value of either thought so limited or the forms of speech which embody such a doctrinal position. To have faith is not to possess or be possessed by an automatic activity; the life of faith is a way of accepting human limitations in the light of revelation which does not do away with them but makes them not only bearable but acceptable as the framework within which human maturity is achieved.

CHAPTER SIX

THE ESSENTIAL UNTIDINESS

Never get things too clear. Religion can't be clear. In this mixed-up life there is always an element of unclearness. . . . If I could understand religion as I understand that two and two makes four, it would not be worth understanding. Religion can't be clear if it is worth having. To me, if I can see things through, I get uneasy—I feel it's a fake. I know I have left something out, I've made some mistake.[1]

TRUTH is a way of looking and a way of talking about what is seen. To speak truthfully is possible because of the truthful man's self-discipline which enables him to say what he has to say without giving false impressions. The truth or falsity of a statement lies largely in its overtones and undertones, for they make the atmosphere in which listeners are influenced by the actual words spoken. The minister of the Word, of course, cannot manufacture the undertones and overtones of his utterance for the occasion, they are spontaneously generated as a result of years of interior activity. These powers that quicken speech are born through the interaction of prayer and thought and do not act automatically; they cannot be summoned, they come to crown all genuine attempts to speak the truth in love. This means that ministers of the Word must always be alert lest the implications they make are other than they intend, though their chosen words may appear adequate when submitted to tests suggested by use of the dictionary.

Ministers of the Word must frequently recall that what they do when they are not speaking to people makes their speech truthful.

[1] Baron Von Hügel, quoted in the Introduction of *Letters from Baron Friedrich Von Hügel to a Niece*, edited by Gwendolen Greene, J. M. Dent & Sons, 1928, p. xvi.

In solitude they are given sufficient coherency to speak with the degree of lucidity and the kind of precision which their subject permits. Coherency is God's gift; he gives it freely but it can only be received by those who preserve an untidiness of mind. The tidy mind is not the truthful mind; the utterance that leaves no room for doubt or place for question is the fruit of a mind that is full of unwarranted conclusions. To think truly, to speak and act truthfully, to avoid the manifold dangers of 'schizophrenia' a minister of the Word must deliberately preserve an untidy mind. This untidiness of mind will irritate him, he will often be weary of living in what seems a mental muddle. At times he will be terrified, he will fear for his sanity, he will dread the loss of his self-respect or of his humility; generally his respite consists in the realization that to bear the burden of this muddle is the true way of preserving real knowledge.

The foregoing paragraph is not meant to imply that the acceptance of human finiteness leaves a truthful minister of the Word tongue-tied or incomprehensible whenever he speaks. He is capable of comforting and admonishing in language that can be understood; but he cannot give the exact details that so many long for, nor dare he offer clichés to the hungry sheep. For their sakes he sanctifies himself, he preserves the muddle, the untidiness of his mind. To speak the truth is to be more than a purveyor of pious information: it is to show the way to think and not to offer the results of thought; it is to sharpen a man's perception rather than to tell him what to see; it is to describe to him the love of God but not to define it.

God looks at the universe of men and things, he looks at it steadily and he sees it whole. Man, made in the image of God, can look at the universe of men and things, he may look steadily, but he cannot see it whole. The conclusions of his thought, therefore, are tentative; of necessity there are factors which he has left out and there are factors whose existence is hidden from him. In fact it is confusing to speak of the conclusions of human thought, for by its nature it is inconclusive. God became man without ceasing to be God so that men might be godly without ceasing to be men; the God-Man Jesus Christ reveals to men sufficient knowledge of the nature of God and of man for the fulness of human thought and love and life. But temptation remains: frequently we would be as gods knowing and explaining all, that is, we are tempted to make our minds tidy. The description of the vocation of a minister of the Word is clarified by considering the necessity to keep his mind untidy. He is not one who has all the answers (or who knows all the relevant questions), he is one who has the way of answering that leads to further questions. In answer to the question Where is God? the minister must talk about the immanence of God in all things and persons and corporate movements of persons. God is the meaningfulness of what happens when people meet to break bread and to pray; without him there would be neither bread to break nor prayers to form. God is the meaningfulness of what happens when men unite to discover truth in committee, laboratory or law court. He is in all things, all things are in him, yet God is more than the sum of his works, he does not express the whole of his being in his ceaseless activity. God is both immanent and transcendent at the same time. The minister of the Word begins a line of thought from the fact of God's immanence; he continues that line until he is about to deny God's transcendence, then he begins a line of thought from the fact of the divine transcendence but must bring it to an end before he finds himself in the position of denying God's immanence.

The question about immanence and transcendence leads to others. We do right to exult in the creative activity of God through rejoicing in nature, art and science—but what of the crooked narrow street, with its smells, decayed masonry and lean, pale children? What about brothels, drug-peddling, crowded prisons and cities like deserts where men and women lose themselves? What about bribery and corruption on the grand scale with truth and justice treated like commodities to be bought and sold? What about the mass-produced daydreams masquerading as literature and art? In answer a line of thought must be started from the fact of human freedom and continued until divine omnipotence is about to be denied, then a line of thought must be started from the fact of divine omnipotence and continued until human freedom is about to be denied. These two lines of thought cannot meet in a point to provide a solution of the problem of evil. Their value lies in that they do provide a way of seeing the reality of human responsibility more clearly and of recognizing that God's omnipotence is most fully discernible in the seeming inactivity which is his active refusal to take away human responsibility because it is the foundation of human freedom and dignity. This leads to a consideration of God's care for people, beginning with the undoubted fact of the value he gives to each individual and then finding that the movements of society sweep individuals about regardless of their separate importance; just as this seems to be the fate of individuals, evidence of consideration given to individuals comes to light and again there must be two lines of thought which cannot meet in a conclusive point without violation of the truth.

A minister of the Word's untidiness of mind is sufficiently enlarged through consideration of the implications of the doctrine of creation to preserve the greater untidiness of mind that is necessary in order that he may preach the mystery of Christ, truly God and truly man, crucified and triumphant. To do this the preacher must consider the humanity of Christ so extensively that he almost loses sight of his divinity; at the same time he must think so profoundly of Christ's divinity that he almost loses sight of the reality of his humanity. In the figure that has been already used, two lines of thought are started from opposite points and cannot be developed far enough for them to meet. To consider this in a slightly different way, devotion must be given to the Jesus of history, but another kind of devotion must be given him at the same time: he must be adored as the eternal one without whom nothing is made that is made, who was before the beginning, who ever will be. These two expressions of devotion do not depend on any finished conception in the mind, they arise from an experience which cannot be represented by any single concept or image.

The minister of the Word is perplexed by the many voices he hears within the Church. He looks for the authority that is decisive. He must, therefore, reason about the Bible and inevitably the line of his thought will move out towards the Body to which the Bible belongs. When he has moved his thought out in that direction as far as he can he finds that it will not meet the line of thought which he is developing as a result of consideration of the Body. In his further search for decisive authority he will discover that his thought about proclaiming the truth of the Gospel does not meet the line of thought he forms from his consideration of the eucharist as a partaking in truth at the behest of him who is the truth and the life. His consideration of authority will lead him to think of the Church and the world. If he begins to think of the Church as the sole agent of revelation in the present he reaches the point where he must reflect on the truths appreciated and expressed in the arts, sciences and philosophy. He has to admit that men and women implicitly or explicitly hostile to Christianity have moulded his development to a certain extent through music, poetry, novels, science and drama. What is more difficult, he has to recognize that he is being influenced by the combined effect made on the whole of society by cinema, radio, television and popular literature. He knows that nothing comes into being without, at least, the divine permission; he knows further that every act of creation is an act of revelation. But there is no ready-made yard-stick by which he may measure the amount of truth in works which have their origin beyond the specific sphere of church activity. For example, he must not be prejudiced in favour of the novel written by a Christian as against the one written by a single-minded agnostic. In a mistaken attempt to be honest he must not be biased against the work of Christian artists and scientists though he bears in mind that some Christian artists and scientists may be 'schizophrenic' and work from a set of assumptions held unconsciously and which are in contradiction to those consciously affirmed in worship and in conversations that are specifically religious.

The minister of the Word's judgment of all works that are *extra ecclesiam* is made with reference to Christian doctrine and by use of his own reason. This can only be truthfully done where there is a truthful attempt to understand the nature of the work being considered. For example, in the case of drama it would be false to decide that a play like Samuel Beckett's *Waiting for Godot* or Arthur Miller's *Death of a Salesman* had a simple discernible message which could be directly doctrinally tested. (The approach to drama as something capable of being taken literally is the outcome of a belief about the nature of reality which makes it inevitable to hold that drama is either a literal statement or nonsense). Good drama, as a Christian sees it, is the exposure of dramatist, players and audience to the truth, while bad drama protects players and audience from the truth as a result of the dramatist's falsification of his consciousness which tends to make him end with a neat conclusion instead of a question mark. Whatever dramatists may learn from preachers, preachers have much to learn from dramatists about the obliquity and ambiguity of dramatic expression, for the statement of truth demands dramatic forms and the masters of drama can help ministers of the Word to discriminate between what is dramatic and what is merely sensational. Every adequate religious statement has an intensity, a proper excitement and an ordered movement which are dramatic, but the ability to achieve this in spoken words belongs to the poet. Perhaps it is that all dramatists have something of the poet in them and all poets something of the dramatist, while ministers of the Word need the power of tense ordered expression which depends on qualities like those of both poet and dramatist. The use of words is a professional matter for the preacher and he should be ready to learn from all masters of words, religious or irreligious, in order that he may better learn how to expose people to the truth. He knows what this exposure to the truth means for him both through his continual pastoral experiences and the tensions of his untidy mind which he will not tidy up in the interests of making decisive statements where none can be made. Orthodox Christianity adheres to the truth of human creatureliness and the reality of its ramifications and regards it as more serious for a minister of the Word to be dogmatic where he should be agnostic than for him to be agnostic where he should be dogmatic. Orthodox Christianity also appreciates the discernment and discretion necessary in the preacher who is forever aiming at saying just enough to be truthful. If he exceeds his authority, whatever his motive, he distorts the truths he would make plain. What he can only say incompletely must be left incomplete, for speech can be no more complete than the thought from which it emanates.

What has been said earlier about the essential untidiness in the truthful minister of the Word could be recapitulated in a geometrical pattern built on a circle. A point on the circumference is marked 'divine immanence', a line is drawn from this point towards but stopping short of the centre of the circle. Another point on the circumference is taken opposite to the point marked 'divine immanence' and marked 'divine transcendence', a line is drawn from it towards but stopping short of the centre of the circle. The gap between these two lines represents the inconclusiveness of attempts to reconcile God's immanence with his transcendence. Other points on the circumference are taken in pairs opposite one another according to their pairings thus: 'divine omnipotence', 'human freedom'; 'the humanity of our Lord', 'the divinity of our Lord'; 'the Bible', 'the Body'; 'sermon', 'eucharist'; 'Church', 'world'. In the diagram no lines drawn from opposite points on the circumference reach the centre of the circle; thus the diagram, with its lines of varying length drawn from opposite points on the circumference making an uneven space round the centre of the circle, represents the essential untidiness of mind of a minister of the Word. The movement of his thought would always follow the pattern indicated by this diagram: the lengths of the separate lines would differ according to the subject of his attention and there would always be an uneven space round the centre of the circle.

To maintain an untidiness of mind results in choosing forms of expression which are often regarded as poor defence against skilled opponents or as inadequate presentation of the Christian position to the faithful and to serious enquirers. But as St Augustine says, 'Let those rage against you who know not what labour is needed to discover the truth, and how difficult it is to avoid errors. Let those rage against you who do not know how rare and hard it is to overcome the imaginings of the flesh by the serenity of a pious mind. Let those rage against you who do not know the difficulty of giving health to the eye of the inner man that he may be able to gaze upon his Sun. . . . Let those rage against you that do not know with what sighs and groans the least particle of understanding about God can be acquired. And, last of all, let those rage against you who have never been ensnared by such an error as they see you to have been ensnared.'[1] In keeping the essential untidiness of mind preachers sometimes fall into the errors which make their utterances indefinite up to the point of meaninglessness or total incomprehensibility. This is less dangerous than the results of the easy fluency of a minister of the Word who assumes that all the words he uses should and can be unequivocal. But the language can be no more tidy than the thought out of which it springs; that is, untidiness of mind makes for ambiguity of expression.

The tidy-minded ignore the fact that it is an error in human thinking to hold that for every word a man may use there is an unchanging entity to which he can point and say, 'When I use this word that is exactly what I mean, no more and no less.' To use words like man, character, will, personality, disappointment is not to speak unequivocally because there are no entities exactly corresponding to man, character, will, personality, disappointment.

[1] St Augustine, *Contra Epistolam Manichaei quam vocant fundamenti liber unus*, ii, 2 included in *An Augustine Synthesis* arranged by Erich Przywara, S.J., Sheed & Ward, 1945, p. 79.

These words never could be unequivocal because they refer to complexities which cannot be reduced to single definable terms. Untidiness of mind could only be banished at the expense of truth; silence would be the only way to avoid ambiguity in speech. If there were an attempt to make conversation as unequivocal as possible, those taking part in it would have to restrict themselves to such remarks as: 'There are three books on the table', 'The cat is on the mat', 'This jam is red', 'That picture is three feet by two'. But ambiguity is accepted in everyday speech: a man is not accused of being untruthful if he says 'I love apples' and then destroys one of the things he says he loves by eating it. When a man says 'I'm always thinking of you' the girl does not reply 'Liar', she says 'And I love you too'. The acceptance of ambiguity in everyday speech is unconsciously made, but consciously there is often an insistence on the use of plain definable terms whenever anything of importance is discussed.

There is an old saying that when we like we liken. We hope by the use of comparison to achieve precision in description and thus it is that the use of analogy is born out of a desire for the degree of accuracy which may be hoped for in accordance with what is being described. The accuracy of our speech can never exceed the accuracy of our knowledge of the particular subject discussed and the limitations of our knowledge in general. Our most accurate statements are always the nearest approximations that can be made. It is our perennial temptation to make a practical denial of the finiteness of human knowledge in an attempt to tidy up our thinking so that we can make unequivocal statements about matters great or small. We are continually making analogies, or using them, and assuming that we have made a literal statement of fact; this is specially so when the language used is not that normally associated with poetry. Thus we are inclined to consider that when someone says 'Follow Christ' the injunction is a simple literal direction indicating exactly a pattern of activity which both speaker and listeners understand in an identical way. The disunity of Christians is apparent whenever they discuss the practical consequences of obeying this injunction. Some non-Christians and nominal Christians will agree that it can have no practical consequences because no one knows what it means. The Christian says that the injunction 'Follow Christ' has practical consequences which, for example, lead one man to change his occupation, another to work more diligently where he is, another to spend more time in solitude. The injunction will make as many implications as there are people and thus it never can be considered as a simple definable instruction to be directly applied by every man in every situation. The minister of the Word can say, as St Peter said, 'Repent and be baptized'. 'Repent' does not refer to some activity to which the preacher can point and say 'This is precisely what I mean when I use the word repentance'; he cannot define exactly what it means to be baptized yet he can say a great deal that is significant about both repentance and baptism. Each single statement made about repentance or baptism is an attempt to give an indication of its nature; the prudent minister of the Word avoids the appearance of offering a literal description where only an analogy can be made. His intentions are often misunderstood, for reasons which Robert Graves describes in a quotation made by C. Day Lewis—'. . . the educated reading public has developed analytic powers which have not been generally matched by a corresponding development of the co-ordinating arts of the poet. . . . The analytic spirit has been, I believe, responsible both for the present coma of religion among our educated classes and for the disrespect into which poetry and the fine arts have fallen.'[1] What Graves says is true of a large cross-section of the community: there is a common notion that the only real mental activities are concerned with analysing and proving; there is a corresponding notion that to present a statement which is not meant to be a proof or something capable of analysis is no more than frivolous. Neither the poet nor the minister of the Word can say what he has to say in unequivocal analysable sentences. Austin Farrer describes what both attempt: 'We write in symbol when we wish our words to

[1] C. Day Lewis, *The Poetic Image*, Jonathan Cape, 1947, p. 113.

present, rather than analyse or prove, their subject matter. (Not every subject matter; some can be more directly presented without symbol.) Symbol endeavours, as it were, to *be* that of which it speaks, and imitates reality by the multiplicity of its significance.'[1] Christian symbols have lost their evocative power for many of those modern people who have grown up in the Christian tradition, while for large numbers who have grown up outside that tradition these symbols never had evocative power. The analytic spirit is strong, but it has led to the analysis of the principles of analysis and we have reached a stage when the ability to analyse is questioned because the principles of analysis are so uncertain that the processes they guide seem in the eyes of many to be meaningless. Thus the minister of the Word is dealing on the one hand with old-fashioned rationalists and on the other hand with irrationalists, or potential irrationalists. He has to safeguard the validity of reason without encouraging rationalists to fancy that he is denying the reality of mental processes other than discursive reasoning. He has to help to establish confidence in mental processes other than discursive reasoning, without lending support to the irrationalist's notion that discursive reasoning is obsolete. He has to protect people from turning to religion in order to buy premises cheaply so that they can go back into the trade of thinking again. He has to protect the devout from welcoming the breakdown in secular thinking as the beginning of a condition where religious revival may be expected. For when the secular way of thinking breaks down the proclamation of the Gospel becomes no less difficult and its acceptance no more likely than in a time when men believe in the reliability of their manifold powers of thought. The movements of society as a whole have had their repercussions within the Church, though it must never be forgotten that what happens within the Church has a profound effect on the whole life of society out of all proportion to the numerical size of the group of practising Christians.

The Church presents the premises on which life and thought

[1] Austin Farrer, *A Rebirth of Images*, Dacre Press, 1949, pp. 19-20.

can be based and demonstrates the scope of the thinking these premises encourage and the style of life they engender. The Church says to everyone born, 'Your vocation is to be human and the way to be human is to be a Christian.' This is said mindful of the strange notions which are widely held as to what being human means, and the strangeness of the notions must determine the way the Church's ministers begin to proclaim the truth that sets men free to be men. But further, the strange notions widely held in society about the nature of man shape the feelings, the thoughts, the aspirations and the temptations of church members; church membership does not give men and women immunity from the mental states and spiritual diseases of their generation nor does it cut them off from the benefits of every proclamation of truth wherever that proclamation is made and by whoever it is made. So it is that now within the Church the uncertainty of society is reflected in the uncertainty of theologians. For we are concerned with the doctrinal question that springs out of the mind of our age: Can the Christian way of life be expounded in unequivocal terms? This leads to the further question: If you say that the Christian way of life can only be described in ambiguous terms are you not turning faith into credulity and discrediting significant mental processes at a time when men are losing confidence in their reality? The minister of the Word who asks himself these questions and sets about answering them will be on the way towards attaining the confidence and coherency that are appropriate to the proclamation of the Gospel both in the pulpit and out of it. He will then be prepared to accept the fact that every attempt to be unequivocal fails not only on account of the subject matter but also because people's minds are more apt to work by association than in argument; one thing reminds them of another in an arbitrary, unpredictable way which is not conducive to good listening in the case of a sermon in the form of a sorites. The effective speaker is always more concerned with making the appropriate allusions than with trying to ensure that the steps of his argument will move logically towards their proper conclusion.

This recaptured wisdom about the working of the human mind has made both ministers of the Word and artists look for ways of talking to their fellows with greater precision, as they understand precision. Their attempt disturbs and angers one section of society and moves another to admiration: in the literary sphere Yeats, Joyce and Eliot are still regarded either as eccentrically incomprehensible or as the leaders in a new age. In the religious sphere there are those who find parables an offence (unless allegorically treated), and all statements not literally true out of place in serious discussion, but there are those who through the current movements in science and art are seeing more clearly what happens when one takes seriously both the reality of the divine revelation and human creatureliness. The sciences and the arts have taught much about human creatureliness. Modern scientists do not claim to be able to give a literal description of the universe; they will say that the most accurate measuring and weighing are no more than the nearest approximations. Poets hold that they never mean exactly what they say because they cannot say exactly what they mean. Artists explain that the painter cannot step out of a landscape and paint it as a detached spectator producing a picture which is to be marked correct or incorrect as a child's sum in arithmetic is marked.

The statements made by a minister of the Word are as ambiguous as those made by artists and scientists whose work helps him to understand that all his doctrinal statements are approximate and untidy descriptions of reality and to see the difference between imprecision and ambiguity in a realm where precision means the choice of the most appropriate analogy. In this light a minister of the Word also sees, for example, that statements about the eucharist are not to be regarded as correct or incorrect but judged rather as attempts to affirm God's immanence in the eucharistic activity without denying his transcendence. The completely satisfactory doctrinal utterance would be a group of statements which made such a gesture that the unity of doctrines was indicated in the movement of pointing to the significance of a particular human experience. That would be a height of precision which could only be reached by the deft use of ambiguity. They who could hope to attain such precision are those who maintain the untidiness of mind which is essential to a faithful minister of the Word.

CHAPTER SEVEN

WHAT IS COMMUNICATED?

PEOPLE are more interested in attitudes than principles. They long to have an attitude that will prevent them from being lost in the major human experiences of love, hate, treachery, betrayal and death. A small number are specially concerned to be able to bear their doubts about the significance of what they are doing in the classroom, in their struggle to master words to make verse, at the laboratory bench, in the stillness of a church made quiet through much prayer. In all this there is the realization that the right attitude and the strength to maintain it are the things most to be desired in life, for what could be better than to be confident?

Confidence is not a thing that can be taught or given to another by a donor's act of will. Confidence is assimilated by a process that is largely unconscious and held by thinking and acting confidently rather than by too prolonged and too intense reflections on its nature. Confidence, like happiness, eludes those who deliberately look for it but is given to those who give themselves over to the pursuit of something other.

Ministers of the Word are called to live with such confidence that they forget all about their confidence and only then can they impart it to others. When confidence is forgotten it is manifest in the manner in which a preacher says what he says. 'He makes you feel better' the uneducated will say, and their criticism often means 'he helps you to have and to keep the right attitude'. That he can do this depends on

> something given
> And taken in a lifetime's death in love,
> Ardour and selflessness and self-surrender.[1]

[1] T. S. Eliot, *Four Quartets*, Faber & Faber, 1944, p. 32.

The ardour and selflessness and self-surrender consist in keeping the essential untidiness of mind which makes possible the study and practice of technique fitting for the truth of what is to be said. As thought about the mysteries of the Christian faith must be untidy, the language which expresses the thought must also be untidy in the sense that it must be ambiguous. To preserve an essential untidiness of mind and to talk ambiguously with un-swerving confidence, loving the truth more than the results of speaking it—that is a description that can be made of a faithful minister of the Word. To accept the fragmentary nature of human knowledge develops the simplicity of a mature man. Simplicity is neither irritated nor indifferent because human deeds and human words are not fully understandable even to the agent; the attempt to confine oneself to unequivocal deeds and words is a naïve gesture made against the realities of life like a child's game of make-believe. No man makes his own maturity, but after its dawn childish language, understanding and speaking must come to an end. No one can make another mature but men can help one another towards maturity by giving constant attention to the ambiguity inherent in all use of language, and this is the special professional concern of the minister of the Word. He is most likely to inspire confidence when he himself is confident and when the form of his utterance expresses his confidence. This can only happen when he is working continually to find ways of saying accurately what can only be said ambiguously. Frequent consider-ation of the necessity of being ambiguous leads the minister of the Word to reflect both on the nature of what he is to communicate and on the sermon as a means of communication.

To preach is a profound necessity for the preacher's own development. A preacher's interior life must be expressed in appropriate overt acts or it degenerates into a delicate private soul-culture. Preaching is one of the most significant activities by which a preacher gives freely what he has been freely given. In the giving he grows and in the growing he communicates to others that which the use of words alone could not convey. Once a

73

sermon is made it is given a life of its own which lives in all who hear it and in the man who made it. In making a sermon the preacher makes something he cannot control and whose future he cannot predict, for no human act is under the complete control of the agent. Once performed a human act affects the whole of humanity through the men and women who experience it immediately. Thus every sermon is addressed to the whole of humanity and is mediated through those present at the preaching of it. It is important to consider that the effect of a sermon on anyone, on any group, cannot be described in purely intellectual or purely emotional terms. There is no such thing as an 'appeal purely to reason'. People do not attend if they do not feel interested, that is if they are not emotionally moved. Some talk about a teaching sermon, or a sermon on doctrine, implying that its purpose is to offer information in as workmanlike style as possible. But burden any sermon with instruction and it ceases to have sharpness and power. Every sermon worthy of the name is instructive, but it is much more because the Gospel is more than a lesson to be taught and learnt. There is no such thing as a teaching sermon that is purely intellectual in its aim and results, nor can there be a sermon which is purely an emotional appeal; mere excitement, no matter how strong, dies leaving little behind it except a thirst for further excitement. The truth spoken movingly is a sowing, and in time the fruit ripens, but there can only be proper sowing when preachers school themselves to remember that there is always one thing more important than the attempt to move people, and that is the attempt to speak the truth in love. The effects of a sermon need to be described in both emotional and intellectual terms as there is no state of mind which is either purely emotional or purely intellectual. Whenever a man listens to what another says, the more significant the utterance, the more complete the listener's response, and the greater his difficulty in realizing what is happening to him. He will be aware of an intensification of his feelings as well as a multiplicity of thoughts which he cannot force into a pattern. The greater the sermon the less listeners will be inclined

74

to talk about its exact effects on them. People are generally bored by sermons they understand too easily and are moved by those they do not fully understand.

Listening to a sermon is like attending to a work of art. To attend to a work of art is not to share an identical experience with the person who made it. If you were to talk to him about your experience of it he would be surprised at the significance you saw in his work and he would be amazed at the intentions you imputed to him. The poet gives his poem a title as the merest guide to those who pay attention, but not in an attempt to arrange that all who pay heed may see and feel only what he wishes them to see and feel. To examine a work of art is always to examine yourself; to know a work of art is to know yourself, though, paradoxically, it is only possible to know a work of art if you know yourself. Knowing is here used not so much in the sense of acquiring factual knowledge as in the sense of acquaintanceship. To be acquainted with yourself is to be at ease with yourself in recognizing the manifold movements of thoughts and wishes within you and to be ready to extend the area of consciousness through the experiences that make this extension possible. Attention to a work of art is one of the experiences which extends self-awareness; the height of this attention comes where there is the intimacy of acquaintanceship which T. S. Eliot describes in speaking of

'. . . music heard so deeply
That it is not heard at all, but you are the music
While the music lasts.'[1]

In the case of preaching, preacher, congregation and sermon are one while the preaching lasts, and in their unity the divine power moves, affecting them in ways that can be neither commanded nor foretold.

Our Lord came that we might have life and that we might have it more abundantly. In modern terms, he came that we might enlarge our consciousness; to resist the enlargement of consciousness

[1] T. S. Eliot, *Four Quartets*, Faber & Faber, 1944, p. 33.

75

is the refusal to have life and have it more abundantly. He is the truth, he frees us from sightlessness and narrowness, he saves us from being held in the web woven by thoughts and wishes that circle round a single point of interest small enough for a kind of safety but not big enough for life. He who is the way, the truth and the life must be accepted as the truth before he can be the way and the life; the fulness of life he offers must be accepted before the truth which he is can be perceived and the way he shows followed. Sermons, like works of art, can have the effect of extending the consciousness of both preacher and congregation, making demands on the hearers as exacting as those made on the preacher. There is need, perhaps, for much thought on what might be called the ministry of hearing beginning with a study of what happens when even one person gives active attention to a sermon.

A sermon is an art-form because to preach is to do more than give information. In present usage 'to inform' is to instruct; the schoolmen used 'inform' as a technical term meaning 'to give inner form'. Consideration of these two uses of the word can deepen appreciation of what is done when the Gospel is preached. There can be no proclamation of the Gospel which does not give proper place to historic facts, but facts of another order must be stated before the relevance of the historic facts can be made clear To say that Jesus of Nazareth was executed during the governorship of Pontius Pilate is the statement of one kind of fact; to state that his death is an essential part of his redemptive work is to state a fact of a different order. Acceptance of the first fact is possible through satisfaction with historical evidence; apprehension of the second can only be made in faith, and no man can give another faith by an act of will. The preacher is to keep on expressing the truth in as intelligible and imaginative a way as he can at the time of each utterance, remembering that like poet, painter, musician. dramatist he changes his function and rôle if he attempts to bully, flatter or cajole. Like them he is to believe in the attractive power of his art and thus avoid the ways of a salesman who makes extravagant claims to give people what they want at a price they can easily afford. At the same time the minister of the Word is to beware lest he make honesty his idol and judge himself on his success in being cryptic—no true artist deliberately paints riddles for the sake of being obscure, no true poet thinks his integrity depends on the choice of images which none but the few can interpret.

What is communicated when a sermon is preached? If the answer could be given in a formula then there would be no need to make sermons. What Miss Helen Gardner says when she writes of the art of T. S. Eliot might well be considered by ministers of the Word: 'It is not the poet's business to make us believe *what* he believes, but to make us believe *that* he believes. He must convince us that he is himself convinced. He must also convince us that what he believes genuinely interprets, makes sense of, experience which we recognize as our own. Although we may not accept his interpretation, we must feel it is a real interpretation. In an age like ours, with no accepted system of belief, in which the traditional system is not so much actively disbelieved as ignored, such an interpretation can only convince if the poet forgoes what earlier Christian writers loved to employ: the language of the Bible and of the common prayers of the Church. The problem of communication for a religious poet in an age where his religious beliefs are not widely held is a special aspect of the general problem of communication for the poet in the modern world.'[1]

It is not the preacher's concern to *make* people believe what he believes, though he cares very much what they believe. It is not his first concern to make Christian doctrine clear; his first concern is to illuminate life, to be a living agent in the process of enlarging his hearers' understanding of themselves by dealing with human experiences in such a way that those who attend to what he says will consider themselves as being directly addressed. Great preaching, like great poetry, deals with love and death, with life

[1] Helen Gardner, *The Art of T. S. Eliot*, Cresset Press, 1949, p. 68.

77

and birth, with hate and treachery in such a way that something significant is said about the tragic aspect of human life. Human life must first be seen as tragedy before the Christian interpretation of human triumph can be appreciated. Our Lord says, 'Your sorrow shall be turned into joy', that is, a man is not relieved of the burden of sorrow, but it is transformed by his bearing of it. It is only by means of doctrine that the preacher can interpret the experiences of life; conversely, doctrine cannot be adequately proclaimed and accepted where there is not sufficient meditation on the characteristic and inevitable human experiences. In looking at preaching from this viewpoint, what de Burgh says of a work of art enlarges on what is being said here about preaching: 'The greatest works of art seem to possess a mysterious power to reveal the inner meaning of the universe, a power of which all must be conscious, but which none but the poet can express in words without vagueness and banality. . . . As a living writer has put it, such works "are not self-contained, but point beyond themselves" as if the experience could lift the spectator "to a height from which he could contemplate all time and all existence, or as if the artist in creating them had tried to pack into his recalcitrant material of sound or colour or language all the incalculable mysteries of the universe or of the human mind." . . . Art is able to call into clear expression the dim background of human consciousness in contact with the dim background of reality.'[1] The last sentence in particular describes the primary task of the minister of the Word whether he is preaching a sermon, joining in conversation with others or whether he is with one person who has come to him in elation or despair. Miss Gardner says that the poet must 'convince us that what he believes genuinely interprets, makes sense of, experience which we recognize as our own'.[2] The attempt to do this becomes possible by profound introspection which discloses the common ground of human experiences in a way that eludes the outward glances intent on making an analysis of the situation.

[1] W. G. de Burgh. *The Life of Reason*, Macdonald & Evans, 1949, p. 77.
[2] Helen Gardner, *The Art of T. S. Eliot*, Cresset Press, 1949, p. 68.

Abstract analysis hides the main truth that introspection clarifies, namely, that a man is not a spectator of the movements of society but a participant who has a share in making the situation which partly conditions him. Thus the preacher is never in the position of one who is talking 'to them about their experiences', he is one who shares communal experiences and he can never do that if his approach is that of a statistician or an analyst. That is, the minister of the Word is to be fully alive himself if he is to help men and women to interpret their experiences; whenever he attempts to avoid experiences that are inevitable or whenever he does not try to make sense of those experiences which endanger the balance of his inner organization, he loses his power to convince men and women that he is able to interpret life. Doctrine that is not consistently applied atrophies or seals itself in a compartment of the mind, producing the conditions in which theological 'schizophrenia' flourishes. A master of the minister of the Word's art has given the injunction: 'Bear ye one another's burdens and so fulfil the law of Christ.' He sets another injunction beside it: 'Let every man bear his own burden.' Any preacher is trivial or incomprehensible if he is not bearing his own burden—an artificial one will not do. The preacher's power to communicate depends upon his ability to interpret the pain of being human.

> 'They say my verse is sad: no wonder;
> Its narrow measure spans
> Tears of eternity, and sorrow,
> Not mine, but man's.'[1]

The preacher is to be described as 'sorrowful, yet alway rejoicing': he sorrows as one who rejoices; he rejoices as one who is mindful of sorrow both his and man's. Man knows a strange sadness in his most sublime moments and joy even in his despair. Human states are never simple; they have the complexity which Blake knew and showed so clearly when he talked of sorrow and joy being woven closely in the fabric of being.

[1] A. E. Housman, *More Poems*, Jonathan Cape, 1936, stanza from the introductory poem.

79

A heightened consciousness and a delicate sensitivity illuminated by faith and illuminating faith develop the preacher's maturity
and free his technical ability from the trammels of stereotyped
forms. The experiences which illuminate the preacher's faith are
not accidental happenings outside his responsible control, they are
fruits of a style of life whose nature is largely hidden but which is
active obedience to the Lord's injunction: 'He that findeth his life
shall lose it; and he that loseth his life for my sake shall find it.'
At the point where a man's individuality seems to be dissolving he
becomes most individual and most powerful in the lives of others.
Faith makes a man strong through hope and vulnerable through
love. Vulnerability and strength are proportionate to one another
and between them keep the preacher's seriousness from becoming
sentimental and his firmness from becoming relentless as he sets
about his task of wounding men with the revelation of their
greatness.

This chapter has offered a sketch of the prerequisites necessary
before a sermon can be effective. All that has been said will fall
into place through reflection on the fact that ultimately the
preacher's work is to help people to be in a state of mind where
perception is possible, that is, in a state where their minds are
open and receptive to the divine action. As Miss Gardner says of
the religious poet, the minister of the Word ' . . . in an age like ours
with no accepted system of belief, in which the traditional system
is not so much actively disbelieved as ignored . . . forgoes . . . the
language of the Bible and of the common prayers of the Church.'[1]
The minister of the Word is not under the full burden of this
handicap in the pulpit, but he must be mindful of it when he talks
to small groups of people and to intelligent enquiring individuals
whose seriousness and spirituality have emerged through their
reflection on their experiences made by principles of interpretation
not easily recognized as religious, much less Christian. The
minister of the Word's art is not in his ability to state Christian
doctrine simply and then apply it to common human experiences

[1] Helen Gardner, *The Art of T. S. Eliot*, Cresset Press, 1949, p. 68.

nor is it his art to talk vividly about human experiences and then show how doctrine makes sense of them; his art lies in his ability to talk about human experiences in such a way that in the same movement of speech he illuminates both human experience and the doctrine which interprets it. It has been said that Christianity is a way of walking, not of talking, and that it is caught, not taught. Talking has power to enlarge a man and without speech Christianity cannot be caught. That is to say, the minister of the Word works to achieve the precision in his utterances which is the poet's power both to be incisive and to extend the range of human consciousness. Not only is he to have the precision of a poet, he must also have the patience of a fisherman. How men are enlarged and caught continues to be a mystery bound up with the mystery of what is communicated when the Gospel is proclaimed. The words in which it is spoken are the words of life and it is not given to the preacher to manipulate them as he wills.

CHAPTER EIGHT

THE USE OF IMAGES

IN the introduction to *New Lines*, which he has edited, Mr Robert Conquest says, 'To be of one's own time is not an important virtue, but it is a necessary one.'[1] Later in the same section of the introduction he remarks that 'Post-war poetry has often been criticized for dealing too much with language, and with the poetic process itself, as though these were in some way illegitimate subjects. This seems rather a superficial misconception: the nature of art and of the whole problem of communication has in recent years been seen as the centre of philosophy and of human life, and perhaps no subject is potentially more fruitful. . . .'[2] Theologians would agree about the potential fruitfulness of study made of the problem of communication and would think no excuse necessary to justify the present preoccupation with the theologizing process and the language in which doctrine is best thought and expressed. In this same volume what Mr. John Wain says of poets of the nineteen-fifties applies also to preachers:

And then there is the question of how far
You can expect the Common Man to share
Your own concern with words and what they are.

The shades of meaning hover in the air,
But when you want to point to one precisely
The others cannot see them glowing there.

You dare not speak too primly or concisely
Because your hearers for their simple needs
Feel that a few crass gestures will do nicely.[3]

---

[1] Robert Conquest, *New Lines, An Anthology*, Macmillan & Co., 1956, p. xiv.

[2] *Ibid.*, p. xvi.

[3] From 'Who Speaks My Language' (iv), by John Wain, *ibid.*, p. 87.

Probably most hearers want preachers to speak concisely and precisely about the mysteries of thinking, loving, living and dying so that all their questions are answered and their unformed questions anticipated. The minister of the Word must not lead himself into falsity through his awareness of the immediate needs of those to whom he ministers, that would be the corruption of compassion; but he must continue the search for better speech which can only be a real search if he also continues to bear the essential untidiness of his mind. Only the truthful can speak truthfully, only the man of integrity is capable of giving others confidence that 'what he believes genuinely interprets, makes sense of, experience'[1] which people recognize as theirs. The minister of the Word's integrity depends on his refusal to deny his creaturely limitations in his attempts to convince others of the reality of divine revelation. He is tempted to give up the essential untidiness of mind which determines the ambiguous nature of his most precise utterances. There are times when the simple explanation, the direct advice in a complicated moral situation, the definite pronouncement about international affairs or industrial disputes seem more necessary than anything else; but the minister of the Word must wait in what seems to be darkness, for prophecy and eloquence are not according to the will of man. They are born in integrity; the moments come when the prophet sees the dim outlines of truth and his eloquence is the ambiguity which points to the many-sidedness of truth, not vaguely but with the precision of one who also knows the single-centredness of truth.

'The Word was made flesh' and men saw the single-centredness of truth. The Word is to be heard through the preacher's words, it is to move with them and in them, it is to be the meaning of their meaning. What words shall the preacher choose and how shall he use them? In present day preaching there is much experiment with new forms; the experiments are chiefly concerned with the use of images and frequently show an insufficient awareness of the

[1] Helen Gardner, *The Art of T. S. Eliot*, The Cresset Press, 1949, p. 68.

connexion between doctrine and the form in which it is expressed. Wise preachers have shown us that form must be tested both by its power to attract attention and by its adequacy to express the fulness of the Gospel; they also teach us that the appropriateness of form does not depend on sheer quantity of matter but on its order and arrangement. Many modern preachers hold that biblical imagery is foreign to the times so they take a Pauline text and deal with it in as exact and abstract a way as possible (Col. 3.11 as the text for a sermon on race relations or church unity would be an example of this). Others take one of the Gospel incidents or parables and declare that it has 'one simple lesson for us'. This one simple lesson is made the basis of an instruction, for example on Christian behaviour or on the nature and practice of prayer. The instruction is usually a connected series of abstract statements in the form of an argument leading to the culminating point of the sermon, the concluding exhortation. Generally the abstract statements are amplified with illustrations drawn from contemporary life. Artistically the blending of abstract prose statements and the poetic use of imagery in a single utterance is a blunder which can lead to such confusion of expression that coherency is lost. When a speaker is confused in his utterance he distorts the truth he intends to present. Bad art is also bad psychology, so that the unconsidered use of illustrations is both bad art and bad psychology. Most people, even educated people, do not listen analytically but are affected by the pattern of imagery in an utterance. This pattern is dominated by the most evocative image in it which is frequently a negative one, for example, the hypocritical churchgoer or the vivid picture of a man before conversion and the insipid picture of him after conversion. It can happen that the illustrations are so fantastic or trivial that a most powerful suggestion is made either that those critics are right who say that Christianity is a fairy tale or that it has no word to say about fundamental human concerns. If illustrations are used they must ring true and they must be big enough for their subject, and it must be remembered that to accompany them with instructions about their meaning and use for the benefit of those who listen is no guarantee that the preacher will ensure that his illustrations will have the effect he wishes them to have. People will remember them but not what is said about them. Images move men more deeply than abstract statements can ever move them except where abstract statements evoke images latent in the minds of listeners.

Sometimes an illustration, or vivid biographical or auto-biographical instance, is used to make a point of contact at the beginning of a sermon or address. This use neglects the fact that the mind commonly works by associations rather than by logical progress from point to point under someone's direction. Thus an illustration about air raids causes hearers to occupy themselves with their own air raid experiences and they will probably take little further conscious interest in the sermon; there is no way to prevent people's minds going off at tangents, there is no way of forcing people to make the kind of associations in their minds which best suit the subject. No attempts should be made to do such impossible things by ministers of the Word who are called to respect the individuality of each person and the inexhaustible meaningfulness of the Gospel. Consider again the type of sermon which begins with an attempt to make a point of contact between preacher and listeners by means of an illustration. First it will be shown to have a special significance for the occasion of the sermon. The preacher then uses the illustration to 'bring home' the meaning of a Christian doctrine to the people. That is, he reduces the image he has made by the illustration to a single unequivocal statement and reduces the complexity of a doctrine to another unequivocal statement and then alleges that the two statements are completely explicable in terms of one another. This treatment of doctrine is part of the current fashion of presenting doctrines separately. But one cannot, for example, discuss the doctrine of redemption without discussing the doctrine of creation, and thus the whole body of Christian doctrine is brought into focus by every exposition of any one particular doctrine. Thus the principle that sermons should be constructed on the basis of using images to attract and plain prose to elucidate is to be condemned on doctrinal, psychological and artistic grounds. In this connexion Dr Austin Farrer writes: 'Exact statement isolates a single aspect of a fact: a theologian, for example, endeavours to isolate the relation in which the atoning death of Christ stands to the idea of forensic justice. But we who believe that the atoning death took place, must see in it a fact related to everything human or divine, with as many significances as there are things to which it can be variously related. . . . There is a current and exceedingly stupid doctrine that symbol evokes emotion, and exact prose states reality. Nothing could be further from the truth: exact prose abstracts from reality, symbol presents it. And for that very reason, symbols have some of the many-sidedness of wild nature.'[1] Imagery elucidates itself before those who have eyes to see; it is capable of opening the eyes of the blind, but to explain it and draw lessons out of it is as fatal to its life as word-by-word analysis of poetry.

The Christian religion can never be presented without imagery. Exact prose could not replace the allusiveness that makes imagery the only precision in proclaiming the Gospel. What could be used to illuminate the Passion other than the imagery of the broken bread, the thirty silver coins, the roar of the crowd, the scourge, the crown of thorns, the Cross and the empty tomb at dawn? What could replace the Parables? Could we do without 'The Good Samaritan', 'The Prodigal Son', 'The Labourers in the Vineyard' and all the others? In the high matters of life a man does not search for truth, he waits expectantly for it; it finds him and he gazes at it. Thus in religion contemplation is a more characteristic activity than analysis; to perceive is more characteristic than to prove and to state more usual than to argue. In accordance with this view what Keats wrote to Reynolds about poetry could be said of preaching: 'We hate poetry that has a palpable design upon us, and, if we do not agree, seems to put its hand into its breeches pocket. Poetry should be great and unobtrusive, a thing which enters into one's soul, and does not startle it or amaze it

[1] Austin Farrer, *A Rebirth of Images*, Dacre Press, 1949, pp. 19-20.

with itself, but with its subject.'[1] In religion the manifoldness of
truth is declared through the use of imagery that stirs the whole
mind into action. This brings us to the point where the preacher's
art is seen to be like the poet's in using words to evoke the images
which move the mind. What is true of poetry is also true of
preaching: the great sermon presents the Gospel images in a way
that does not startle but which commands attention. The preacher
often begins work on his sermon not by constructing an abstract
statement but by reflecting on an image and letting it develop in his
mind as it gives rise to image after image in a connexion which is
not fortuitous but according to the laws of images. Images should
be presented as nearly as possible in the order that they are thought
for there can be no forcing of a connexion between them and
fusion between them does not take place through juxtaposition.
Dylan Thomas's description of his creative method contains useful
advice for those who make sermons; he said: '. . . a poem by
myself needs a host of images, because its centre is a host of
images. I make one image—though "make" is not the word: I let,
perhaps, an image be "made" emotionally in me and then apply to
it what intellectual and critical forces I possess; let it breed another, let that image contradict the first; make of the third image
bred out of the other two together a fourth contradictory image,
and let them all, within my imposed formal limits, conflict. . . .
The life of any poem of mine cannot move concentrically round a
central image, the life must come out of the centre; an image must
be born and die in another; and any sequence of my images must
be a sequence of creations, recreations, destructions, contradic-
tions. . . . Out of the inevitable conflict of images—inevitable,
because of the creative, recreative, destructive and contradictory
nature of the motivating centre, the womb of war—I try to make
that momentary peace which is a poem.'[2] Day Lewis, who makes

[1] *The Poetical Works of John Keats*, with a memoir by John Monckton
Milnes, Edward Moxon, London, 1858, in which a letter from Keats to
Reynolds is quoted, p. xxiv.

[2] Quoted by C. Day Lewis in *The Poetic Image*, Jonathan Cape,
1947, p. 122.

this quotation, says that the method is the opposite of George Herbert's 'whose poems spring from a central image, moving concentrically round it and constantly refer back to it'.[1] From a comparison of Thomas with Herbert it might be right to say that Herbert's composition from a single central image is a possible pattern for sermon-making with Thomas showing the kind of process that follows the holding of that one central image.

It is often said that the biblical imagery is quite meaningless to modern men and women. But consider the primary New Testament imagery. Where is the difficulty presented by imagery connected with the birth of a baby in the stable of an inn? What is completely foreign in all that is conjured up in the mind by the depiction of a man sharing a meal with his friends, a traitor betraying his friend, a weak judge, a crooked trial, power politics, the derision of the successful, the condemned man scourged, spat upon and executed, his surprised friends discovering his tomb to be empty? These are the images that prepare minds for the reception of the many-sidedness of the truth towards which they make their manifold allusions. These images are the images which are concerned with the great human themes, and the use of them always stirs men profoundly. Some might call them the archetypal images. But in doing so it is important to note that archetypes (in Jung's use of the term) are not images but modes of common human experience which are brought to full life when evoked by the appropriate images. All men and women experience treachery and the dread of it, they are stirred by the fact or the thought of birth and death, they are moved by the fact or the thought of enemies. A great many sermons fail for the same reason that so much poetry is minor poetry, the reason being that they do not deal, or fail to deal adequately, with the great human themes of birth and death, of hate and love, of treachery, the struggle for self-preservation and the joy and agony of creative activity. Too often Christian preaching confines itself to the territory of

[1] C. Day Lewis, in *The Poetic Image*, Jonathan Cape, 1947, p. 123.

conventionally respectable thought and experience, extolling morality above holiness, will-power above wisdom, human effort above divine grace and temperance above charity.

Sermons weighed down with instruction and exhortation breed images of inferiority which dominate the minds of those who preach them and of those who attend to them. The Gospel contains within it both instruction and exhortation; its presentation in clear images makes the best teaching possible, that is, when speaker and listeners are not too aware of teaching and learning. In the same way the best exhortation is made when speaker and listeners are not conscious of what is being done. To preach is not to teach a lesson nor is it to give moral exhortation: it is to make a statement which has the power to widen and deepen men's minds, stirring their desire to know and understand, moving them towards the discovery of the resolutions each should form. The preacher does not seek to possess and direct others, he hopes that others may possess and control themselves. To this end he must have a threefold aim: first, to release people from all tautness of mind; secondly, to free them from the dominance of others and so deliver them from the burden of false obligations; thirdly, to prevent or break their dependence on him. In order to do this his language needs to be as evocative through its imagery as it is stimulating in the variety of its rhythms. It can be evocative in its imagery because he gives himself over to frequent and regular contemplation of the truths of the Gospel; it can be stimulating in its rhythms because of the deep confidence that comes from accepting that the untidy mind is the truthful mind and that the untidy mind can only express itself in ambiguous language, rich in imagery. The minister of the Word's imagery is made powerful by his frequent attention to doctrine and to the concrete circumstances of particular men and women. Reflection on the particular gives rise to the metaphor to describe it and out of such metaphor universal images emerge. Images of universal stature cannot be intellectually constructed, they can only be recognized when they appear in the mind and they only appear in the mind that is both expectant and patient.

allow
them
so be
node

The minister of the Word waits in hope for the images that adorn and illuminate his utterance, but he is always to remember that no image, despite its many referents, is ultimate; images can only point towards the mystery that is God. When we speak of him, as speak we must, our most exact precision is no more than the nearest approximation, but this approximation is not made without continuous effort and sometimes it is blessed by the discovery that we have the images we need.

True simplicity in preaching lies in realization of the complexity of the task and in being mindful of the mysterious divine co-operation by which the sermon's images increase in power as they move together within the sermon's unity. True simplicity lies in submitting to the laws of sermon construction, so far as they can be known; only thus can the preacher make a sermon which is a form reflecting the glory of the Godhead it honours by being itself a unity in diversity and a diversity in unity.

CHAPTER NINE

A PERSONAL FORM

Many have original minds who do not think it; they are led away by custom. Now it appears to me that almost any man may, like the spider, spin from his own inwards, his own airy citadel.[1]

EVERY minister of the Word owes a debt to particular ministers of the Word; he always remembers those who deepened his feelings and shaped his early thinking through their sermons and the part they took in conversations. The power of a mind growing in its originality through authentic proclamations of the Gospel frees the young from the deadness of empty conventional feeling and thought. Orthodoxy requires originality in those who express it but it is only by repeated attempts to proclaim what is orthodox that originality is developed. Tillich says, 'A theological system is supposed to satisfy two basic needs: the statement of the truth of the Christian message and the interpretation of this truth for every new generation.'[2] This interpretation is always the creative work of individual ministers of the Word with all the uncertainty and agony that is part of such work. Tillich then goes on to explain the work of the ministry of the Word: 'Theology moves back and forth between two poles, the eternal truth of its foundation and the temporal situation in which the eternal truth must be received.' Eternal truth is not to be adapted to the situation in which it is to be preached, and factors in the situation are not to be consciously neglected in order to make it less difficult to find a seemingly relevant way of speaking the truth to people living at a particular

[1] *The Poetical Works of John Keats*, with a memoir by John Monckton Milnes, Edward Moxon, London, 1858, in which a letter from Keats to Reynolds is quoted, p. xxiv.
[2] Paul Tillich, *Systematic Theology*, Volume 1, Nisbet, 1953, p. 3.

place in particular circumstances. What Fr Thornton says about revelation and contemporary culture further elucidates the task of the minister of the Word: 'Throughout redemptive history revelation has received its outward expression in terms drawn from contemporary culture. Cultures, however, are in one degree or another transitory. For, unlike the major uniformities of nature, they are human adaptions of nature which are liable to lose their relevance and their suitability under the changing conditions of historical development. For this reason a living religion shows its vitality by assimilating itself to successive cultures through the advance of the centuries, whereas a religion with less vitality may become fossilized in a particular form of culture, reinforcing it where it should have broken through to new forms of expression.'[1] The new forms of expression of church life and the new patterns of individual behaviour cannot become meaningful and coherent without the continuous work of individual ministers of the Word to express the truth of the Gospel in the language of the generation. No one learns to speak French by learning the meanings of French words together with idioms necessary for conversation; to speak French one must think in French. If a minister of the Word learns his theology in the language of a generation not his own, he must re-learn it by thinking it and speaking it in the language of his own generation. The language of a generation grows out of its faith, its disbeliefs, its preoccupations, its anxieties, its achievements, its amusements, its hopes and its fears. Great ministers of the Word have always preached in a way that is both peculiar to themselves and to the times in which they preached. What they say so aptly for one special occasion is for all occasions; it is characteristic of such preachers that in dealing with the particular, what they say has universal application, and in dealing with the universal its particular relevance becomes apparent. Though a great sermon is made at one point in time it is for all time; though its language may have an archaic ring its significance is clear, because it deals

[1] L. S. Thornton, *Revelation and the Modern World*, Dacre Press, 1950, p. 288.

with perennial human concerns and can therefore be recognized as significant at any time.

No one can preach in the language of a former generation or in any style that does not belong to him without giving the impression either of his own insincerity or the unreality of his subject. The minister of the Word is called to make forms of speech which are at the same time intelligible to others and peculiar to himself, because a man's language cannot be developed apart from his thinking which feeds and is fed by it. Therefore attention given to sentence construction develops both clarity of speech and originality of thought, for there can be no thinking without the formation of sentences as 'thinking is mental discourse, and no act of discourse can be performed without at least two terms. The sentence, not the single word, is the proper expression for thinking.'[1] The sentences a preacher forms in his thinking come into spontaneous use whenever he speaks of fundamental human concerns; thus significant speech is always the overflow of significant thought. But to what is the preacher's thought to be directed if it is to be significant? Allen Tate suggests an answer in what he has written about the man of letters: 'He must first do what he has always done: he must recreate for his age the image of man, and he must propagate standards by which other men may test that image, and distinguish the false from the true. . . . He must discriminate and defend the difference between mass communication, for the control of men, and the knowledge of man which literature offers us for human participation.'[2] If the minister of the Word is to recreate the image of man for his age he must first recreate the image for himself, achieving lucidity in his inner discourse as he considers the Christian revelation of man as a creature made in the image of God yet finite and sinful. But this consideration must be made in full recognition of the ways in which he is conditioned by the preoccupations of the society in whose life he participates.

[1] Austin Farrer, *The Glass of Vision*, Dacre Press, 1948, p. 74.
[2] Allen Tate, *The Man of Letters in the Modern World, Selected Essays, 1928-1955*, Thames & Hudson, 1955.

The preacher's lucidity of mind is only made when he gives due regard to the framework for thinking which doctrine provides and to the immediate needs of a particular generation. Perhaps it is that now the most immediate needs are first met by a clear presentation of what the theistic position involves and of what may be taken as a corollary, namely, that though the individual's freedom is limited yet human behaviour is significant and at its most meaningful whenever there is an attempt, through whatever medium, to express a knowledge of reality that cannot be communicated in unequivocal terms.

Whether a minister of the Word preaches extempore, from notes or full manuscript he will need to write a great deal. Sentences are the units of thought and he needs to make his sentences coherent if his thinking is to be so. Few people can manage this without much secret trial and error in writing. The most useful writing a minister of the Word does is for this purpose and not directly intended as part of preparation for a sermon or conversation. As thought becomes clearer, speech becomes more nearly appropriate for the truth the man wishes to express and the expression becomes more characteristic of him, because the rhythm of his thinking gets into the rhythm of his speaking; 'you don't devise a rhythm, the rhythm is the person, and the sentence but a radiograph of personality.'[1] The minister of the Word's practice in sentence structure is as necessary as the pianist's five-finger exercises and both can hope for reward.

In this century the short sermon has arrived as a new art form. Already work has been done to indicate the way a preacher sets about making the form; there are brilliant exponents of it and others who are capable of occasional brilliance. It is much more a personal form than the long sermon, for the short sermon depends greatly on the preacher's selection of subject matter, his use of figures of speech and his command of words: this command of words, we have been seeing, depends on the preacher's work at sentence structure. Like the short poem, the short sermon must

[1] Marianne Moore, *Predilections*, Faber & Faber, 1956, p. 3.

make its effects quickly and proportionately. Neither poet nor preacher may linger over one movement, each must dispense with every superfluous word while the speed of the movement of the whole and the necessary economy of words makes metaphor more apt for use than simile. Simile needs more words than metaphor and slows the movement of the mind, for in simile the mind has to move from side to side and may fail to return, whereas an appropriate metaphor sweeps the mind along with it. Biblical literature and modern usage both accustom ministers of the Word to metaphor. Habit has trained us to see the forcefulness of such use of metaphor as:

'Ye are the salt of the earth: but if the salt have lost its savour wherewith shall it be salted?'

'Ye are the light of the world. A city set on a hill cannot be hid.'

There can be no speech without imagery, but it must be remembered that metaphor makes its images sharply and quickly. Therefore in a short sermon or a short poem care must be taken about the quantity of imagery used and the potential power of one image compared with another. Any piece of speaking or writing is not merely so many sentences and paragraphs but so many images, and images do not stay in the order that they are spoken or written: the image on which coherency and power depend may come in the middle, at the end or the beginning of what is expressed. Always it is to be remembered that the spoken word depends more on the vividness of its imagery than the written word and that the spoken word is in constant danger of becoming a riot of images whereas the written word has methods of keeping its house of images in order. For this reason great sermons are like great poetry in their control of metaphor and imagery, and for this reason what Day Lewis quotes about a poet's use of metaphor also applies to a preacher's use of it: ' "I think," says Mr Herbert Read, "we should always be prepared to judge a poet . . . by

95

the force and originality of his metaphors." Another critic, Aristotle . . . was equally prepared to put his money on it: "The greatest thing by far is to have a command of metaphor. This alone cannot be imparted by another; it is the mark of genius." [1]

No one can teach another to have a command of metaphor and no man can teach himself to have it, but he can set about the work which prepares him to receive the mastery that he can neither demand as a right nor buy with effort. This work appears to have three main activities: first, training oneself to observe the metaphor of others either in their speech or in their writings; secondly, observing the scarcity of adjectives in great literature (for example the fourth gospel); thirdly, writing descriptions of experiences without the use of adjectives. This third activity is helped by the first two and develops an aptitude for metaphor, but 'command of metaphor . . . is the mark of genius' and genius is not an infinite capacity for taking pains nor is it the inevitable reward of faithful labour but it cannot be given where there is no persistent work. The work done to acquire at least some ability with metaphor helps in the practice of the art form of the short sermon. A short sermon, of course, is not a few carefully chosen pearls put haphazard before the minds of listeners; the pearls are to be carefully arranged and strung so well that the string is not visible. The choice of the string and the threading of the pearls are the personal work of the preacher.

The short sermon is a much more personal utterance than the long sermon and the short sermon preached to a small congregation is still more personal. Here artificiality, or the appearance of artificiality through technical deficiencies, has a profound effect. Here the sermon that depends for its effect on illustrations or on the preacher's reminiscences causes discords of which the preacher may never be aware. There are listeners who look on illustrations as an escape from the rigours of thought either for the preacher or the congregation and many are upset and embarrassed when

[1] C. Day Lewis, *The Poetic Image*, Jonathan Cape, 1947, p. 17.

the preacher is personal in the wrong way, that is, when through illustrations he divulges or appears to divulge intimate biographical or autobiographical details. He seldom hears of the upset and embarrassment he causes on these occasions, but comment is made and people are slow to confide in one who talks too much about those to whom he ministers even when he does so in the most general and anonymous terms. A preacher should use all his personal experience to speak movingly about common human experiences. The sensitive man who has been betrayed will talk about treachery in such a way that people will be enlarged by what he says, especially when his utterance is an exposition of the Passion of our Lord. All a minister of the Word's experiences in living help him to understand more fully the doctrines by which he interprets them and in that sense his exposition of them is highly personal. Sermons are personal in the right way when each listener feels that as a result of the sermon he understands himself better and sees more clearly the individual response that the Gospel demands from him. To hear a minister of the Word preach often should not be to know him better but to know yourself better and only to increase in your knowledge of him through what you realize he has shown you about yourself. That happens when a preacher is working to develop a personal form as he takes to himself the kind of advice that Bishop Jeremy Taylor gave to clergy of his generation: 'Do not spend your sermons on general and indefinite things, as in exhortations to people to get Christ, to be united to Christ, and things of the like unlimited signification. . . . For generals not explicated do but fill people's heads with empty notions, and their mouths with perpetual unintelligible talk; but their hearts remain empty and themselves are not edified.' For example, people should never be continually exhorted to communicate more frequently, but eucharistic doctrine should be presented to them in such a way that eucharistic imagery is apt to be in their minds moving them and making it more possible for the minister of the Word to discharge a pastoral duty in the spiritual direction of his flock one by one. People should seldom

morals

prayer

be given moral exhortation in sermons, but doctrine should always be presented in such a way that the kind of behaviour that expresses Christian belief will be obvious. People should never be urged to pray more, but the doctrines that illuminate prayer should be preached and the kind of devotional practices described which are suited to modern conditions and modern minds. In all these and in similar instances no attempt should be made to give the kind of advice in public which can only be given individually. At the same time doctrines should never be alluded to unless they are being presented and when they are presented the principles by which they are translated into life should be made as explicit as may be. The elucidation of these principles is the bulk of the minister of the Word's work in the pulpit, in the confessional, in classes and conversations. He must work in solitude to achieve a personal form of speech, which though clearly his own, calls attention not to himself but to the many-sidedness of the truth of the Gospel.

Like the poet the minister of the Word has to be able to express himself in a variety of forms and be sufficiently master of all of them not to be self-conscious in the use of any of them or wrongly impersonal, that is, saying in exactly the same way what scores of others say. Perhaps conversation taxes his art more than anything else. In it he has either to respond to the lead made by someone else or he has to take the initiative and talk in such a way that a state of mind is likely to be promoted in others which will be conducive to their greater depth of feeling and width of thought. His first concern is not to begin a specifically religious conversation, but to initiate a conversation about human concerns in a way which will tend to make specifically religious thought inevitable and likely to lead to a specifically religious discussion there and then or on some future occasion. The minister of the Word should not be deliberately startling though he often finds as Wordsworth did that 'a multitude of causes, unknown to former times, are now acting with a combined force to blunt the discriminating powers of the mind, and, unfitting it for all voluntary exertion, to reduce it to a state of

almost savage torpor'.[1] He says later in the same paragraph, talking
about the people of his day: 'the uniformity of their occupations
produces a craving for extraordinary incident which the rapid communication of intelligence hourly gratifies' as the minister of the
Word also knows. At the same time there are other situations where
the higher level of general education is clearly seen and demands
are made on him which test the flexibility of his thinking and the
durability of the inner coherency which enable him to deal with
unexpected questions. Conversation needs forms more flexible
than those dictated by the necessity of preaching short sermons to
small congregations. The varying subjects in a conversation allow
no stereotyped forms of speech; the various people with their
different interests, occupations, education make the development
of a suitable vocabulary a necessity, but to develop a vocabulary
is more than a matter of finding an idiom to replace the one out-
dated. If ministers of the Word are to express themselves through
a modern vocabulary many of them will need to relearn their
theology by thinking it and speaking it in the language of this
generation. This can best be done through giving serious attention
to contemporary drama, novels and poetry, for here will be found
the most likely means of discovering the best language to speak of
the mysteries of life and death in terms that are true to the minds
of modern ministers of the Word and their people. Through
reflecting on the metaphors used in drama, novels and poetry one
can perceive the nature of the concerns, the anxieties and hopes of
contemporary men and women and often find a mirror that reflects
the movements of one's own mind. To live and think solely in an
ecclesiastical and theological mental atmosphere is to be in danger
of assimilating a style of thought and developing a pulpit diction
which falsifies doctrine and is either unintelligible even to regular
churchgoers or a familiar jargon to which they can listen unmoved.
Great ministers of the Word are those who disturb their hearers
into thought and lead them into the territory that borders on both

[1] William Wordsworth, *Prefaces* in his *Complete Poetical Works*,
Macmillan, 1888, p. 851.

presumption and despair where love, joy and peace are to be found.

The use and purification of language is the lifelong work of the minister of the Word. This task entails persistent efforts to use both current and biblical metaphor in such a way that modern men and women may feel and see the truth in a language that depends more on images than on abstract statements.

CHAPTER TEN

SOME OBSERVATIONS ON THE MODERN SITUATION

> . . . I want to be cured
> Of a craving for something I cannot find
> And of the shame of never finding it.[1]

IT is said that art should be either in the fashion or leading it. That is, art should be dealing with the actual feelings and thoughts of contemporary people or else leading them to understand the common human experiences which are moving them at a particular time. Art in speaking profoundly to men at one particular time speaks to men of all times; it is at once modern and timeless. All this could be equally well said about the ministry of the Word. Ministers of the Word are called to be modern; but there is no recipe for modernity, no straight path to it, no simple thing a man may do to make himself modern. Modernity grows out of a man's love for his fellows; it grows out of love for himself as one of God's creatures; it grows out of love for every manifestation of the ceaseless divine activity in the changing human environment. We cannot stop life to watch it, we can only reflect as we live it; this ability is an indication of human greatness but it can provide occasion for the folly of human pride. The individual can make no complete picture of the modern situation; reflection on it does no more than give materials for a partial description. Robert Graves's poem 'In Broken Images' contrasts two ways of thinking and what he says about broken images expresses the principles which govern these observations on the modern situation:

> He is quick, thinking in clear images;
> I am slow, thinking in broken images.

[1] T. S. Eliot, *The Cocktail Party*, Faber & Faber, 1950, p. 123.

IOI

He becomes dull, trusting his clear images;
I become sharp, mistrusting my broken images.

Trusting his images, he assumes their relevance;
Mistrusting my images, I question their relevance.

Assuming their relevance, he assumes the fact;
Questioning their relevance, I question the fact.

When the fact fails him, he questions his senses;
When the facts fail me, I approve my senses.

He continues quick and dull in his clear images;
I continue slow and sharp in my broken images.

He in a new confusion of his understanding;
I in a new understanding of my confusion.[1]

To look at the situation is to examine what is going on among different groups of people and order one's thoughts, as far as they can be ordered, remembering that human confusion of mind is the state of one who sees without fully seeing, knows without fully knowing and never completely understands what he knows. Society is never in such a condition of uniformity that its members can be described *en bloc*, nor ever so atomized that only a description of individuals one by one would be of value. Society cannot be divided into a series of groups, each to be treated as if it had a life of its own independent of all other groups; groups are continually affecting each other both directly and indirectly.

The words duty, conscience, guilt are rarely heard in present day conversations (except when guilt is used as a legal term); their occasional use seems almost anachronistic. The disuse of these words is taken by some as a sign that all sense of moral responsibility has gone. Some religious people hold that the decline of religion in society has led to a deterioration in morals. Other religious people answer by claiming that many modern immoral people are unconventionally religious and many conventionally

[1] Robert Graves, 'In Broken Images', *Poems, 1926-1930*, Wm. Heinemann, 1931, p. 40.

religious people are immoral on account of their irresponsible attitude towards the present movements in society. Of course there is widespread irreligion and moral irresponsibility is common, but at the same time there are religious longings and moral aspirations which are not easily recognizable by those whose consideration of human behaviour evokes only the images and concepts that emanate from the words duty, conscience, guilt. Modern people do not use these words, the serious do not think about behaviour in such terms. They do not look at life as movement from one simple moral situation to another where the issues are always clear. They are bewildered because they see that their choice is so often plainly between two evils and that so many significant human deeds must be performed when there is no time for deliberation; they are disturbed by uncertainty of motive and they dread hypocrisy. Modern people feel that there can be no pragmatic test of action in an unstable world and that where there is no single established culture intelligible behaviour is impossible. There is little danger of smugness in responsible modern people; on the contrary they are so unsure and so uneasy about the value of what they are doing that they often lack the stability that feeds and is fed by mature human action. They are haunted by the same kind of doubts that are the agony of artists: at one moment it seems futile to master a technique when there is nothing to be expressed through it; at another moment the thing seen seems so rich and complex that no form could ever be subtle enough for its utterance. Modern people feel as unable to help one another about questions of behaviour as poets are to help one another about the making of poetry. One poet can do very little for another in the quest for words to give outward form to the rhythm that is the mind's obsession. In the same way it is felt that while there are technical skills that can be learnt to equip one for human behaviour no one can teach another either to recognize the subtle difference between one human relationship and another or to perceive the demands made on the participants in a relationship and the nature of the appropriate responses. A modern man, for example, would not think of himself as sure that he has done his duty to his wife or that he knows precisely what his duty to her is, or that he could be told in detail by anyone else. ⟩

One of the strengths, and at the same time one of the weaknesses, in this period is concentration on personal relationships which is making them more and more difficult for Christians as well as for nominal and non-Christians. At the beginning of this century responsible people were ready to sacrifice the well-being of personal relationships for the furtherance of their life-work; now the tendency is to sacrifice too much for the well-being of relationships. Whenever the maintenance of a human relationship becomes an end in itself it puts such a strain on all concerned that it either breaks or continues at a high spiritual and psychic price paid in large instalments by those who devote themselves to the making of the relationship. The Gospel advice ‘He that findeth his life shall lose it and he that loseth his life for my sake shall find it’ has an obvious application to individuals sharing relationships. It could be put in this way: They that seek their lives together shall lose one another and they that lose their lives together for the sake of the Lord shall find themselves in him. A hard saying and an incomprehensible one to all who look for fulness of life entirely within the sphere of human relationships. The ability to maintain relationships depends on a belief about what being human means; from this belief follows the discovery of ways in which those who share a relationship help one another to be human. A minister of the Word can say these things easily enough but in the middle of the twentieth century he has to remember the kind of people who think he could not say anything wise or pertinent to them in their struggle to live significantly for the sake of those they love.

In our day people do not generally think and speak of moral responsibility in terms that have been long familiar; hence within the Church the question, expressed in one form or another, is often asked, ‘In what does moral responsibility consist and how should I discharge my responsibility in this particular situation?’ The answer can only be given according to what is believed about the nature and mode of revelation. Advice given with regard to conduct shows the variety of beliefs consciously or unconsciously held about the nature and mode of revelation. In church circles there are those who speak of conduct as a matter of separate acts performed by isolated individuals, estimating the value of what is done without much serious consideration of the situation in which the acts were performed. Other voices are heard making judgments on deeds done, or giving advice as to what should be done, with a definiteness only possible where those who speak assume a knowledge of all the factors which constitute a situation. Others claim that every moral problem is capable of being solved through the unequivocal direction given through prayer. Others reduce every question of behaviour to a matter of family duty, offering guidance by advising consideration of one's place in the family as son or father, mother or daughter, uncle or cousin, and so on. The theology of many ministers of the Word makes it impossible for them to give positive detailed advice about behaviour in a complex situation. They will offer to help others to make clear to themselves the general intentions which a man should be attempting to express in every situation, they will help him to see as many aspects of any situation under discussion as they themselves perceive, but they will leave the means of expression to the individual's own discovery. This attitude in ministers of the Word gives occasion to all sorts of misgivings and doubts in the minds of those who consider either that the man of faith should have all knowledge of all things or that each human situation is capable of a simple explanation because all human acts are capable of a literal interpretation. Whenever ministers of the Word will not give detailed instructions about behaviour and are as slow in approving without qualification as they are in disapproving without qualification, many Christians are inclined to take up the attitude that all standards of behaviour are purely relative, or else they will turn to those who give the plain advice that can be given by those who have made an implicit, or explicit, denial of the finiteness of all human knowledge.

The question for many modern people, Christian and non-Christian, is not about moral behaviour but about meaningful behaviour. Are human speech and action significant? If I cannot know what I want to do, and if no one else knows what he wants either, can it matter what I do or leave undone? We are at the stage when the difficulty about deeds is becoming as widely realized as the difficulty of language. It used to be held fairly commonly that a man might have trouble in expressing himself in words, that the religious might expect to find that the irreligious could not follow what was said to them about religion, but that all could understand the meaning of a religious man's deeds. 'Actions speak louder than words' was a favourite saying. The modern man is apt to say 'Actions speak louder than words and are just as bewildering. Who can prove their meaningfulness when no satisfactory demonstration of the reality of human freedom and purpose can be made?'

This attitude towards behaviour expresses the spirit of an age in which sections of people are in a post-atheist state. In these sections a man does not ask himself 'Do I believe in God?', but 'Do I believe in belief? Do I believe that coherent living and thinking are possible?' If nothing can be taken as axiomatic there can be no interpretation of experience, no knowledge of self, no knowledge of others. Indeed even the axiom that there can be no axioms must be rejected. In this period he who thinks deeply, Christian or non-Christian, has to re-examine the basis on which his thinking rests: 'Beginning to think is beginning to be undermined. Society has but little connection with such beginnings. The worm is in man's heart. That is where it must be sought. One must follow and understand this fatal game that leads from lucidity in the face of existence to flight from light.'[1] For the Christian, 'lucidity in the face of existence' must not lead to 'flight from light'; he is to remain in the light that dazzles but does not destroy, learning there that every advance in human knowledge means an increased awareness of the extent of human

[1] Albert Camus, *The Myth of Sisyphus*, Hamish Hamilton, 1955, p. 12.

ignorance. Modern psychology makes modern people question motive as an interpretation of any action, modern sociology and modern philosophy make them distrust pragmatic evaluation of an action; modern physics makes them realize that their control over their bodies and all other matter is partial and not fully understandable. The Christian can rejoice in this state of affairs because, for him, the terms in which limited human knowledge is expressed are symbols of humanity's splendour as well as of its limitations. He knows that the symbols of fifty years ago must be put away without regret because now others are needed to express a new knowledge of God and of himself. This is not because God adds to the truth—he expresses the truth in full but humanity grows in perception of this fulness. Humanity grows as an individual grows and the growth is not to be described in moral terms but in terms of an increased understanding of human control over matter and of the significance of human relationships. Obviously the present extension of knowledge is dangerous both to religious and irreligious people. The religious are tempted to think that new knowledge is not relevant to living or to cling desperately to religious symbolic statements made in an age they describe as 'an age of faith'; they may consider themselves to have lost their faith, whereas what has happened is that they have abandoned a fixed system of thinking which could not remain fixed if serious attention were given to new facts of experience. A readiness to pay heed to new facts of experience, even when they seem to endanger the religious view of life, brings with it a condition of uncertainty that is often mistaken for doubt in the existence of God because it is clearly seen that the meaningfulness of every new fact is not immediately apparent to the human mind. The present extension of human knowledge is dangerous to the irreligious; their perplexity can lead them to accept as axiomatic that there can be no question of talking sense about life because there are no real grounds for either believing in or doubting the significance of human thought and action. This is not a state that people can be argued out of; for them the acceptance of despair

consequent on the realization of the meaninglessness of human
life is taken to be the achievement of human maturity. This
attitude makes the Christian look again with searching eyes at his
own thought about maturity. To be mature, according to Christianity, includes a recognition that all human knowledge is partial
and that much human sin arises out of resentment against this
human limitation.

Those who live the post-atheist style of life are not of course
only to be found among the reflective. They are to be found on the
golf-links, in queues for cup-ties, waiting to be served in the
grocer's, whiling away endless hours over tea or in the bar. The
pattern of their behaviour shows their assumptions. They rarely
mention religion except to say that it is a thing that a handful of
women, children and eccentrics go in for; church attendance is
never mentioned as an alternative way of spending part of Sunday.
They enjoy those popular forms of entertainment and literature
which never openly attack religion but ignore it.

Society always needs rebels and owes much to them. They draw
attention to what the conservative and the conventional should
but do not wish to see; they protest when the form of society
ignores the rights of the individual in the interests of efficient
social life or when favoured individuals are valued more than the
maintenance of justice in communal life. The right kind of rebel
will protest when either statutes or customs hinder the development of men and women according to their proper ambitions and
the inspiration of their particular genius. A settled society dreads
change and persists in encouraging a type of behaviour which was
socially useful at one point of the society's history long after that
point has been passed. What is true of society as a whole is true of
the Church: we do not easily give up types of piety and spirituality
which were noble and courageous in their day but which have
become obsolete. Within the Church rebels make protest against
stereotyped utterances, thought-forms, patterns of piety and
spirituality. Rebels merely become impatient or eccentric if they
do nothing but protest; they are prophetic when they indicate the

thinking, the spirituality and the piety which would most adequately express the timeless at a particular point in time. Emmanuel Mounier says that, 'It is the heavy responsibility of books of theology and spirituality intended for the general public, as well as of sermons, that they annex sacred history, misunderstanding its rebirth in each one of us, and too often transform the call to adventure in the life of the Church into the recital of an inventory.'[1] Rebels within the Church must always bear in mind both the torpid and the rebellious outside it. Churchmen sometimes speak as if the whole of the community outside the Church were throbbing with life and stimulating profound thought in the places where one would expect to find profound thought. They speak like that when they deliberately, or indeliberately, give the impression that there is some swift or sure way of increasing the vitality of the Church to match the imagined vitality outside it. It is urgent to have scrupulous regard for truth in making an exhortation of this sort and to make it clear that there is lassitude and virility both inside and outside the Church. Mounier says, 'It remains to be seen if this manner of dozing beside the thread of fate, and of turning human drama into a family outing and burning problems into a school exercise, is a monopoly of relaxed Christianity. There is a comfortable atheism, as there is a comfortable Christianity. They meet on the same swampy ground, and their collisions are the ruder for their awareness and irritable resentment of the weakening of their profound differences beneath the common kinship of their habits. The prospect of personal annihilation no more disturbs the contented sleep of the average radical-socialist than does horror of the divine transcendence or terror of reprobation disturb the spiritual digestion of the habitués of the midday Mass. Forgetfulness of these truisms is the reason why so many discussions are still hampered by naïve susceptibilities.'[2] A section of English society is atheist and contains those

[1] Emmanuel Mounier, *The Spoil of the Violent*, The Harvill Press, 1955, p. 25.
[2] *Ibid.*, p. 25.

not perturbed by the profound implications of their position; a section is post-atheist and largely unperturbed. But there are those atheists and post-atheists who are deeply uneasy, and like Dostoevsky's their halleluiahs, if they are uttered, will burst out of a furnace of affliction. It is among men and women of this sort that ministers of the Word do some of their most important work, for these are people who are unconsciously religious and unconsciously exert a religious influence on others, including those who minister to them. Much perception and subtlety is required in helping to bring an unconscious state of mind into consciousness. Impatience can halt the process, and at all times direct methods tend to provoke a defensive response. In the end pastoral rapport may be born out of patience and respect for the other's freedom and individuality. There is no substitute for rapport, and where it cannot be established the fact must be frankly admitted.

In modern society feelings of guilt are common, but are called by some other name. A man who feels guilty is out of touch with himself, awkward in his own company, consumed with a need to apologize to himself and feeling foolish, for how could he accept his own apology? Commonly modern people do not accuse themselves of particular wrongdoings but from time to time they are aware of a vague uneasiness about themselves which is the result of many causes, most of them generated unconsciously. English people feel inferior, unconsciously, on account of England's decline in power, and ashamed and a little frightened of an economic situation which appears to be out of control. People feel uncomfortable about the colour bar. They feel uncomfortable on account of the many reminders of prostitution and homosexuality which tend to make them disgusted, or else frustrated because they can discover no way of expressing their compassion. This is one of the frustrations that combine to keep men and women uneasy as a result of the masses of information which make them feel helpless because they can neither understand fully all they are told nor act significantly in response to the urgent demands which the information makes on them. This feeling is characteristic of modern man's lostness in a world that seems to him a maze, a journey without maps or a standing still and waiting without wonder or peace.

In this age when the individual's range of significant activity is seen in its narrowness there is a tendency to consider the domestic sphere as the area within which human activity has its most, if not its only, profound meaningfulness. In fact the family is the one institution that many modern people believe in. This is often an unconscious admission and it can be seen in many speeches by educationalists, social workers, politicians, churchmen, where emphasis on the importance of the family is made by such phrases as 'In the end it all depends on the family', 'family life is the backbone of the nation', implying that let institutions be what they will the family is the one institution which is capable of significant action and has power to influence the lives of people. On account of the small family now so common and the well-fostered regard for family life, members of a family tend to over-examine one another and get on one another's nerves or live a stylized life with all the current family ritual and ceremonial. Family life is good, not bad, but a man's life consists of more than meticulous fulfilment of family obligations (see Matt. 10), and a Christian protest must be made against tendencies to act as if any human institution could demand absolute loyalty from its members. The protest has to be put into words, but before that can be done it must be expressed in a style of life. Wherever a man is creative he will be jealous of his liberty, he will go to any length to be himself and refuse the rôle an institution may try to foist on him; a man of spirit will not submit to be ordered what he is to feel and think, whether the orders are given in church or home; he will refuse, he will behave in as opposite a way as he can. At the beginning of this century the rebel against institutions became an atheist and an upholder of free love because Church and family stood for his enslavement. Now in this post-atheist period the denial of the family is the one effective proclamation of freedom, but what was technically known as 'living in sin' is not the boldness that it was fifty years ago. The boldness now is the homosexual relationship; this relationship should never be treated merely as a matter to be explained in terms of sex. It would be rash to say that there is more homosexuality now than at any other time, but the present common attention to homosexuality is significant and shows the atomized nature of English society through the groups represented by various spokesmen on the subject. The homosexual relationship is described as a social protest, a moral degeneracy, an unforgivable sin or the only romantic attachment left. Ministers of the Word are not called to condemn or condone; they are to be compassionate, and compassion means a width of outlook as well as keen perception. Compassion never loses sight of man as a responsible agent nor as a participant in the movements of society which so often dazzle, bewilder and terrify him as he makes his attempts to be himself and no other man. To be oneself is the adventure of living; to accept this adventure is to accept darkness and danger in discovering that human knowledge is fragmentary; it is to find that human certainty looks frail and that human motives are always mixed. Ministers of the Word deny the truth of the Gospel when they equate the good news with a message about morality. In fact the use of the word morality at this point tends to confusion when modern man desperately needs to see that there is such a thing as meaningful human behaviour. He is looking for the sort of assurance that Celia in *The Cocktail Party* needed; she says:

> . . . I want to be cured
> Of a craving for something I cannot find
> And of the shame of never finding it.[1]

Like many modern people she could find her state more bearable if it were merely a matter of being cured herself; she says:

> But first I must tell you
> That I should really like to think there's something wrong
> with me—
> Because, if there isn't, then there's something wrong

[1] T. S. Eliot, *The Cocktail Party*, Faber & Faber, 1950, p. 123.

With the world itself—and that's much more frightening!
That would be terrible. So I'd rather believe
There's something wrong with me, that could be put right.[1]

These observations on the modern situation are no more than
the equivalent of the sketches an artist makes before painting.
Each minister of the Word in the end must draw his own sketches
and paint his own pictures of the modern situation. He will have
to make countless sketches and no single picture will satisfy him,
for his knowledge of himself through self-examination and his
growing knowledge of the lives led by others, individually and in
groups, will cause him frequently to modify the conclusions he
comes to about the pattern of communal living. 'Now we know in
part' and partial knowledge only permits tentative conclusions but
tentative conclusions are sufficient for meaningful speech and
action.

[1] T. S. Eliot, *The Cocktail Party*, Faber & Faber, 1950, p. 117.

CHAPTER ELEVEN

MODERN APOLOGETICS

In the pulpit the best apologetics are the clearest presentation of the Gospel which ministers of the Word can make. This presentation should emphasize God's deeds rather than man's needs. Without God's ceaseless activity men would know neither their needs nor themselves, without reflection on his ceaseless activity there could not be the wonder that leads to worship.

If the Gospel were a set of propositions then the language of apologetics, in and out of the pulpit, would depend on a mastery of prose, but if the centre of the Gospel is a person then the language of Christianity must have a marked dependence on poetry. To be poetic is to make a deliberate use of words not intended to be taken literally but chosen as the best that can be found to present the complexity of a subject of unlimited meaningfulness. Thus the following words addressed to those who would be poets is matter for reflection for ministers of the Word who would be apologists: '. . . you can never be a poet unless you are fascinated by words—their sounds and shapes and meanings—and have them whirling about in your head all the time. Above all the poet develops his poetic faculty through contemplation—that is to say, by looking steadily both at the world outside him and the things that happen inside him, by using all his senses to *feel* the wonder, the sadness and the excitement of life, and by trying all the time to grasp the pattern and help others to grasp it too.'[1] The preacher knows that the pattern is not completely discernible, for mortals cannot see either the beginning or the end of things, but in the light of revelation it is possible to see the movements of life from their beginnings towards their end. 'I am Alpha and

[1] C. Day Lewis, *Poetry For You*, Basil Blackwell, 1944, p. 35.

Omega, saith the Lord, the beginning and the end'; all human thought and speech begins in him and ends in him. Day Lewis says to the poetry reader, 'If you're afraid of having your feelings stirred in the way poetry can stir them, if you don't want to see more of this world than meets the eye, if you're afraid to see beyond your own nose, then you would certainly avoid poetry. . . .'[1] The same could be said to those who would listen to the proclamation of the Gospel from the pulpit or out of the pulpit, for it is terrifying to be presented with the implications of human knowledge and the extent of human ignorance. 'Poetry is a special way of using words,' says Day Lewis, 'in order to create a special effect upon the reader and to light up the world for him. . . .'[2] Preaching is also a 'special way of using words in order to create a special effect upon' those who listen and 'to light up the world for them'. How is this done? Reflection on a further remark of Day Lewis's gives indications of an answer: 'Poetry must put part of you to sleep in order to wake up another part of you. It puts to sleep the part of you that reasons and argues, it awakens the part that remembers, feels and imagines.'[3] The nurture of the mind is assimilated by use of the powers of memory, feeling and imagination before the clarifying work of reason begins; in stressing this fact Einstein said that the imagination is more important than intelligence, meaning that there can be no meaningful use of intelligence unless there is imaginative perception.

The presentation of the Gospel gives rise to questions and the apologist must be ready to deal with them, and the bulk of his apologetic work will be done out of the pulpit rather than in it. He will be questioned by men and women who want to test the truth of what he says in the pulpit in the light of their experience. People will want to know whether the discoveries of modern scientists invalidate the Christian doctrine of creation; they will want to know whether the work of psychologists conflicts with the Christian conception of man; they will want to know whether

[1] C. Day Lewis, *Poetry for You*, Basil Blackwell, 1944, pp. 1-2.
[2] *Ibid.*, p. 1.　　　　[3] *Ibid.*, p. 31.

Christians consider that the arts express an authentic knowledge of reality. But most commonly the apologist will be asked about the way in which Christian belief can be expressed in the individual and group behaviour of people in modern society. Some of those he meets want a security that can be maintained without strain and without effort. In some form or other the minister of the Word will be asked either to interpret the Gospel in terms of behaviour or behaviour in terms of the Gospel because serious men and women are concerned with the problems that arise out of their thinking, speaking or acting and expect that Christian doctrine is capable of illuminating these problems, or otherwise they consider it has nothing to do with life. The apologist will meet many who want none of the things he considers essential to life and who will frame none of the questions he is ready to deal with. In the case of those people he will do all he can to stab them into an awareness of themselves and they will generally resist his attempts with every psychic power they possess, but he must continue with subtlety and patience, the subtlety that makes oblique approaches and the patience that keeps hurry and aggression in check.

> . . . truth, like love and sleep, resents
> Approaches that are too intense.[1]

People resist those whose approaches to them are too intense but always tend to be moved by those who respect them; the apologist must respect the integrity of others as much as he respects his own.

Every sermon is apologetic but in present conditions many of the most significant apologetic tasks are outside the pulpit and to perform them the minister of the Word needs much wisdom and skill in dealing with small groups of people and with individuals. It requires one kind of ability to talk to a congregation of two hundred and another to take part in a conversation with four others and yet another to help a solitary individual to put into words what he finds it extremely difficult to put into words. It

[1] W. H. Auden 'New Year Letter' from *Collected Longer Poems*, Faber & Faber, 1968.

requires much restraint to leave a man with his broken sentences rather than let him misrepresent himself by using words directly given him. Attention given to individuals separately and to small groups is a powerful means of suggesting the importance of the individual at a time when so many are questioning their own significance. The apologist does well to reflect on the importance of giving this attention but he should never make himself too conscious of his purposes when he takes part in a conversation. He leads a conversation best who submits to the conditions in which it takes place, remembering that the most profound religious conversation can develop out of discussing a subject that is not specifically religious. When he is alone he can by his thinking develop an attitude towards his work out of which may be born the unselfconsciousness which puts others at their ease and the carefreeness that infects them with a love of life (an anxious apologist is the incarnation of a contradiction). No man can make this unselfconsciousness and this carefreeness; they are the gifts of God who makes the single-minded strong with the beauty and power of faith, hope and charity.

There can be no stereotyped methods of apologetic: all depends on perception of the nature of each particular opportunity and an adherence to a general policy in apologetic work. In the nature of things this general policy cannot be elaborated in detail, for it must be flexible if it is to be implemented in the separate unique circumstances that constitute the field of apologetic work. The following paragraphs are a suggestion towards the formulation of a general policy left with a deliberate indefiniteness, because finally each individual apologist must adapt any policy both to his immediate situation and to his own bent and temperament, for in this personal work a policy cannot be a blueprint; if it is to be effective it must be neither so loosely formed that it is vague nor so tightly knit that it strangles initiative.

In modern apologetics consideration of theism must often precede consideration of christology and attention must often be given to the implications of the doctrine of creation before

presenting the doctrine of redemption. Those who do not accept
the Christian doctrine of creation cannot accept the doctrines
of the incarnation and redemption. The modern apologist frequently finds that he is dealing with people who need, first and
foremost, to discover what the Church's doctrine of creation is.
In many cases he must be ready to expound what being religious
means and what being monotheistic means as a prelude to his
exposition of Christianity. Creation should not be presented as past
event but as continuous activity, for God is to be presented as the
creator of all the stirrings in the human mind as well as of the
shifting clouds and the song of the birds. He is to be presented as
the maker of machines and of the flowers in the man-made
gardens and the fruits of man-tilled earth. His creative work is to
be recognized in the bread on the breakfast table and in the consecrated bread on the altar. In drawing attention to the ceaseless
creative work of God it is necessary to run the risk of appearing to
be pantheistic—statements lose the fire of truth when their
movement is slowed down by qualifying parentheses. Often
reflections on creation, for doctrinal and psychological reasons,
stop short when the Christian thinker finds that he has led himself to a position where he must consider the mystery of evil. But
he must not stop, he must recognize the divine operation manifest
in the works of artists, Christian and non-Christian, in the prayers
of the devout, in the construction of aircraft and high explosives,
for without God nothing is made that is made. This will bring
difficulties in plenty but nothing like the confusion that comes
from reluctance to deal with all that is implied in the fact that
nothing can be brought into being without the divine assistance.
It must be admitted that the concentration of the forger and the
perseverance of the man of prayer both depend on the divinely
created energy.

It is important to reflect on the mystery of goodness as well as on
the mystery of evil. A poet cannot tell how he made the perfect
line; genius cannot be taught and it is only the flash of genius
which gives lustre to all behaviour, whether the poet's in making

verse or the hero's in magnificent disregard for his safety. In the sphere of human relationships there are no rules to be found for knowing the appropriate behaviour in a particular situation. No ethical code could have made it obvious that the breaking of the alabaster box of precious ointment was fitting to a strange occasion. The roots of human behaviour are mysterious and are partly seen, not so much in making and carrying out decisions as in the spontaneous response made to sudden demands or unexpected opportunities. This is not to say that great behaviour is achieved without work, but that the necessary work is not the outcome of following simple instructions. The Christian says that the glory of human behaviour is the result of a combination of human labour and divine inspiration and that no one can will the moment of his inspiration because all creative human deeds are possible only through God's ceaseless creative activity and no man can command its expression at a particular time or at any time. Reflection on the mystery of goodness (where goodness means more than and yet includes the common conception of goodness in specifically moral terms), leads men to wonder and wonder can be the beginning of religion; thus part of the apologist's task is to stimulate wonder. It is the mood of our generation that most of us are led to wonder through a balanced view of human achievement which in Christian terms means a contemplation of God manifest in human behaviour. To achieve this balanced view means that a man must sooner or later accept realization of the brutality, the banality and the callousness of self-seekers as part of human experience and that he must accept himself both as a person of mixed motives and unpredictable behaviour and as one whose acts performed with good intentions have sometimes results which make him doubt both their goodness and his power of judgment. Allen Tate makes remarks that are apt for pondering in this context: 'I believe that it was T. S. Eliot who made accessible again to an ignorant generation a common Christian insight, when he said that people cannot bear very much reality. I take this to mean that only persons of extraordinary courage, and perhaps even genius, can face the spiritual truth in its physical body. Flaubert said that the artist, the soldier and the priest face death every day; so do we all; yet it is perhaps nearer to them than to other men; it is their particular responsibility.'[1] The Minister of the Word is frequently instrumental in the breaking up of the illusions by which men protect themselves from the harshness of too much knowledge, and the destruction of their illusions seems to them as death. The apologist must steel himself and help others to steel themselves to put away childish things in order to be men. There is an innocence that is characteristic of the child's ignorance of life and there is an innocence which a man is to achieve in the face of his knowledge of good and evil if he is to see the truth that frees him to be himself. T. S. Eliot's well-known sentence applies to the apologist and to all who pay heed to him as well as to the poet: 'But the essential advantage for a poet is not, to have a beautiful world with which to deal: it is to be able to see beneath both beauty and ugliness; to see the boredom, and the horror, and the glory.'[2]

The work of an apologist can be partly described as that of having an influence over people, and an influence is not something that anyone can will to have or plan to use in specific detail. The following paragraph from a letter gives wise advice to a mother who has reason to be concerned about her son and it is advice by which all who are concerned for others may profit: '. . . I am sure that you can hope to be treated as an "equal friend", if you will deal with the self-pity and gradually give up wanting to be "of influence". True influence can only come as a result of relationship, and only where the relationship is not desired *in order to exert influence*. . . . So long as one needs people as badly as you once needed Alastair, one is bound to try and hold them by being useful to them. . . .'[3] 'True influence can only come as a result of

[1] Allen Tate, *The Man of Letters in the Modern World, Selected Essays, 1928-1955*, Thames & Hudson, 1955, p. 99.

[2] T. S. Eliot, *The Use of Poetry and the Use of Criticism*, Faber & Faber, 1933, p. 106.

[3] Michael Burn, *Mr. Lyward's Answer*, Hamish Hamilton, 1956, p. 214.

relationship'—a relationship is of course not automatically made, indeed relationships are usually established after a mysterious process which is largely unconsciously developed. The deliberate attempt to create an impression, to establish a point of contact or to become indispensable fails except in the case of the over-docile. The most one can do is to be natural about one's own interests, talking freely and undidactically about them, while generally being more ready to listen than to talk, as the other must be given freedom to talk naturally about his interests. Relationships are more likely to be furthered by an interested listener than by an engaging talker, especially if he is bent on using every opportunity to be improving. Through sermons, relationships between the preacher and congregation are made where his utterances are personal in their form in the sense that they are characteristic of him and not dependent on an ecclesiastical diction which hides or prevents the frankness that engenders friendliness. This is also true of conversations where a habitual conventional mode of expression would make a barrier that could not easily, if ever, be broken.

No Christian doctrine should be presented in isolation nor described under a single analogy; the use of more than one analogy is always necessary but there should be a certain emphasis on the analogy that is most apt for a particular generation, and for those of a particular generation who have neither had a theological education nor a specifically religious upbringing. This is of particular point in speaking of the atonement, where a concentration on the sacrificial or forensic aspects of the death of our Lord is a bewildering introduction to the mystery of his atoning work when offered for the consideration of modern men and women. It would seem that the most suitable introduction would begin with an interpretation of his temptations as the urge to do the right thing in the wrong way, that is, to draw men to him at the loss of his integrity by appealing to them through actions they would readily and immediately appreciate but which would make it impossible for him to say, 'I am the way, the truth and the life.'

This generation is impressed by anyone who accepts the whole of his experience and yet continues to act creatively, well aware of the cost to him in the bearing of pain, and modern people are likely to apprehend something of the mystery of our Lord's redeeming work when it is initially presented in such terms. This presentation would need to be amplified by description of the cosmic, timeless nature of all human acts performed at particular points in time; place-bound and time-bound thinking can never do justice to human acts and certainly could not apprehend the significance of the deeds of him who is truly man and truly God. This is no more than the sketch of an introduction to a presentation of the doctrine of the atonement, but the seeds of a proper conclusion may have been sown in it and blossoming may give the conclusion in its full amplification. There are always risks in the presentation of any doctrine, but the presentation of doctrine made in fear of error results in nebulous statements; love of truth is not marked by obscurantist utterances chosen to preserve it but in the unfolding of a mystery under the figure most likely to evoke response. The mysteries of faith are to take flesh in words, and forms of words are very much the creatures of the feeling and thought of a particular time and are parts of the ceaseless creation of God without whom nothing that is could be. If revelation came to an end with the closing of the canon of Scripture, or at any other point in time, then, of course, any consideration of modern apologetics is unnecessary and impossible. But no one can approach Christian doctrine unconditioned by the mind of his generation and this mind does not come into the forceful shape of its being without the divine operation.

The apologist in meeting those who do not practise religion should assume in charity that they do not do so for some serious reason and not take it for granted that they are frivolous or leading a disorderly life. He must try, as he gets opportunity, to help them to understand their reason for not practising religion and the unprovable assumptions on which they base this reason and their way of life. Often an apologist is to help a man to see what is involved in being a conscientious atheist, agnostic or communist. He does this for the following reasons: first, this is the path to truth for the individual concerned and if he is converted he must know clearly from what he has been converted. Secondly, if he is not converted he must be helped to oppose the Church for the right reasons; Christians have a duty to deliver all men from falsehood and folly. Thirdly, the Church is always helped more by intelligent opposition than by deadening apathy. Fourthly, an individual is in a better state if he is helped to oppose truth than if he is left to ignore it; to oppose truth is to give attention to it and that has a saving power which may be resisted but cannot be obliterated. Lastly, when a man sees his position clearly and realizes the axioms on which he is basing his life he may be open for the mysterious activity of the grace of God which none can command but to which all may submit.

The apologist will often be concerned with people who are a long way off from being ready to follow a specifically religious way of life or even to think of doing so. In this situation hurry, impatience and over-eagerness would be the marks of an amateur apologist, and the minister of the Word is to be a professional one whose zeal is not worn away by his patience and whose patience is maintained in spite of imperceptible progress; he must not lose hope when with slow reluctant feet he moves away from the unresponsive one. There is much work to be done and hence much to be left undone in order that something of value may be achieved.

The apologist may use for himself the Pauline analogy between the minister of the Word and the agriculturalist; he has the power to sow and to tend his crops but not to make them blossom and flourish. It may be that he will sow and another reap, but it is enough for him to know that there is a harvest, that all genuine work has genuine results.

CHAPTER TWELVE

WORD AND SACRAMENT

We who must die demand a miracle.
How could the Eternal do a temporal act,
The Infinite become a finite fact?
Nothing can save us that is possible:
We who must die demand a miracle.[1]

THE miracle takes place whenever the Word is spoken and the bread is broken, for these are cosmic timeless acts affecting the entire physical universe and changing the whole of humanity. When these things are done the smallest church becomes an everywhere and an hour becomes a timeless moment. The Word resounds in the words spoken, it is the meaning of the meaning of what is said, it is the power of the release men know when great and terrible truths are spoken, it is the strength of minds delivered from the narrowness of time, it is the mirror in which men see themselves and are saved from the trivialities and folly of their sins. The bread that is broken is the bread of truth and the bread of life, it is the food of the full-grown, 'whosoever eateth of this bread shall never hunger'. Here is no magic but the miracle by which those who must die shall live; this is the temporal act of the Eternal, this is the Infinite becoming a finite fact, this is the moment of full human consciousness—a moment unlike all other moments, a moment when we express our connectedness with all things and all men in God 'in whom we live and move and have our being'. Commonplace words are taken and transformed through the speaking and the listening, common bread is taken and transformed through the blessing, the breaking and the sharing of it. Through the Word spoken and the bread broken the many are given power to be one through the intensification of the

[1] W. H. Auden, 'For the Time Being' from *Collected Longer Poems*, Faber & Faber, 1968.

individuality of each and the sharpening of the identity of each; a scrap of bread broken from one loaf is given to each, the Word spoken is directly addressed to each and yet belongs to all, for all belong to it.

We do not say that the ministry of the Word is more important than the ministry of the sacrament or that the ministry of the sacrament is more important than the ministry of the Word. The two ministries are complementary, rather, two expressions of one ministry. Whenever the minister of the Word prepares to preach he is to remember that he is also the priest at the altar; whenever the priest prepares himself to celebrate the eucharist he must remember that he is also the minister of the Word. His preparation for both consists in all that is entailed in his habitual reverence for common words and common bread. Our use of them is a participation in God's creative work: we take and transform what he forms, so discovering the wonder of human speech and the marvels of human manufacture. In the processes of manufacture man is changed by what he changes. We grow in mind, we grow in understanding of one another, we grow in realization of the powers in the universe which are outside human control. Creative work can be a sort of worship; it can also be a blasphemy: bread can be blessed on the altar or it can be reserved in the market for those who are rich enough to buy it; it can be used as a bribe or a weapon.

Words are created things just as loaves are; the making of them is similar. They are not made without the divine work or without the work of man. Before there can be the perfect order of speech there is the ceaseless human labour in the making of words; there are times when new words are to be brought into language, there are times when technical words have to be brought into common usage, there are times when words, once good, must be replaced because they have become defaced in use. Words are not static things that men make and use like bricks. Words are made in the image of those who make them and use them, showing the marks of human creativity and restlessness, of human nobility and

Words are Powerful

depravity. Words can be used to bless and to curse, to flatter, to intimidate or to manifest the truth through the beauty of rhythm and the pattern of meaning. Words are nurture for the mind just as bread is for the body, and both have their origin in God without whom no thing or word is made and used. God supplies the raw materials out of which words are made, but the transformation of the raw materials is the work of man's imagination, memory, intelligence and determination; the psychic energy by which all mental effort is made is sustained by the ceaseless activity of God 'in whom we live and move and have our being'.

> The Lord who created must wish us to create
> And employ our creation again in His service
> Which is already His service in creating.[1]

In the pulpit and at the altar the minister of the Word takes created things, words and bread, and in their use performs deeds he never fully understands. To take part in the Church's liturgical activity through sermon and eucharist is a participation in events that cannot be defined but only incompletely described. Physical descriptions can be made: a physicist would say that every word spoken sets in motion a minute change in the physical universe which has endless physical ramifications; he would say the same about the breaking of bread in the eucharistic action. A psychologist would make a description in psychic terms; he would say that the very fact of people gathering in one place would cause psychic changes in all of them through the interplay of suggestions consciously and unconsciously given and received. He would go on to explain that what was said alters both the speaker and those who listen in a variety of ways not to be uncovered by a rational analysis of the utterance. He would draw attention to the effect of the spoken words on the whole of humanity through the speaker and listeners. Whenever one man speaks to another, both of them affect all other lives in varying degrees through their corporate act.

[1] T. S. Eliot, 'Choruses from "The Rock" ' from *Collected Poems 1909-1962*, Faber & Faber, 1963.

A psychological description of the eucharist, while drawing attention to certain truths about it, would be equally inadequate; every kind of scientific description would have many limitations. The nature of sermon and eucharist can only be tentatively described; no description could presume to delineate the divine operation in each, which operation cannot be seen within simple terms of discernible cause and effect. In sermon and sacrament we are given what we are too ignorant to desire and unworthy to deserve. Here is not magic but miracle, the Eternal doing a temporal act, the Infinite becoming a finite fact, without ceasing to be eternal or ceasing to be infinite. That is, God acting in time without ceasing to be God in order that men may be godly without ceasing to be men. The Gospel discloses the mystery that this can be, and we are left to wonder and adore, bearing in faith the fragmentariness of our knowledge but rejoicing in its reality.

We are not to live in a closed esoteric circle, we are to be ready to encourage and answer whatever questions men may ask us about the way of life which has its origin and power in sacrament, sermon and Scriptures. Our answers will be as fragmentary as our knowledge and our language ambiguous but used with the precision that is born of faith, nurtured in humility and matured by constant reflection on the truths of revelation. For ministers of the Word this means frequent remembrance of the cosmic timeless acts they are given to perform when the Word resounds in their words, when with frail human hands they break the bread of life in the name of him who is the way, the truth and the life, without whom nothing is made that is made.

INDEX

Aristotle, 96
Arnold, Matthew, 19
Auden, W. H., 51, 116, 124
Augustine, St, 19f., 65

Beckett, Samuel, 63
Blackmur, B. P., 29f., 31
Blake, William, 79
Burn, Michael, 120

Camus, A., 106
Coleridge, S. T., 26
Collingwood, R. G., 20f.
Conquest, Robert, 82

David, 27
de Burgh, W. G., 30, 78
Dostoevsky, F., 110

Einstein, A., 115
Eliot, T. S., 19, 26, 27, 29, 30,
    47, 50, 70, 72, 75, 101, 112f.,
    119, 120, 126

Farrer, Austin, 67f., 86, 93
Flaubert, G., 120

Gardner, Helen, 77, 78, 80, 83
Graves, Robert, 67, 101f.

Herbert, George, 88
Housman, A. E., 79

Jennings, Elizabeth, 34

Joyce, James, 70
Jung, C. G., 88

Keats, John, 86f., 91

Lewis, C. Day, 19, 67, 87f.,
    95f., 114, 115
Lyward, G. A., 120
-
Miller, Arthur, 63
Moore, Marianne, 16, 24, 26,
    94
Mounier, Emmanuel, 109

Paley, Archdeacon, 37
Plato, 26
Pound, Ezra, 24

Read, Sir Herbert, 24, 25, 95
Richards, I. A., 28

Tate, Allen, 93, 119f.
Taylor, Bishop Jeremy, 97
Thomas, Dylan, 87, 88
Thornton, L. S., 92
Tillich, Paul, 91

von Hügel, Baron, 58

Wain, John, 82
Wordsworth, William, 28, 98f.

Yeats, W. B., 70